TRAINING

IMPACT

MEASUREMENT

2023 Edition

TRAINING IMPACT MEASUREMENT

ROI OF COMPLEX TRAINING PROGRAMS MADE SIMPLE

Dr Raman K. Attri

A Publication of Speed To Proficiency Research: S2Pro©

Copyrights © 2021 Raman K Attri and Speed To Proficiency Research: S2Pro©

All rights reserved. No part of this publication may be reproduced, distributed, or transmitted in any form or by any means, including photocopying, recording, or other electronic or mechanical methods, without the prior written permission of the author and publisher, except in the case of brief quotations embodied in critical reviews and certain other noncommercial uses permitted by copyright law.

ISBN: 978-981-18-7257-0 (e-book)
ISBN: 978-981-18-7255-6 (paperback)
ISBN: 978-981-18-7256-3 (hardcover)

Published in Singapore
Printed in the United States of America, Australia, UK

https://www.speedtoproficiency.com
info@speedtoproficiency.com

National Library Board, Singapore Cataloguing in Publication Data

Name(s): Attri, Raman K., 1973-
Title: Training impact measurement : ROI of complex training programs made simple / Dr Raman K. Attri.
Description: Singapore : Speed To Proficiency Research, [2023]
Identifier(s): ISBN 978-981-18-7256-3 (hardback) | 978-981-18-7255-6 (paperback) | 978-981-18-7257-0 (Ebook)
Subject(s): LCSH: Employees--Training of--Evaluation.
Classification: DDC 658.312404--dc23

Editor:
Farheen Malik, Pakistan

A simple yet transformative mindset to move you from the viewpoint of 'return on investment' to 'return on expectations' to make you an influential training business leader

ROI of any training program is simple: when you design and deliver any training program grounded in a sound rationale, business reason, or skill-related need, you just have to demonstrate that you have received the same returns on your "expectations" in the first place.

AUTHOR

Dr. Raman K. Attri is a multifaceted personality with a range of talents, including being a scientist, author, speaker, L&D leader, and artist. His outstanding achievements have earned him recognition as a Brainz Global 500 leader alongside other stellar personalities such as Oprah Winfrey, Gary Vee, Jim Kwik, and Jay Shetty.

Dr. Attri is the world's leading authority on the "science of speed" in professional learning and performance, with over two decades of research in performance science.

Despite being permanently disabled since childhood, Dr. Attri is known as a powerhouse of positivity and inspiration. He has transformed his inability to walk into a unique expertise of teaching people how to walk faster in their professional world.

He is the creator of a time-tested, proven system that can help leaders and organizations to speed up the path to mastery and leadership in any domain by two folds. His most recent project is the GetThereFaster portal, a comprehensive resource for anyone seeking to learn the secrets of learning better and faster.

Dr. Attri is a professional speaker who shares research-based insights at leading international conferences with top business executives, helping them to master speed in business, shorten workforce time to proficiency, and accelerate employee development.

He is also a global training thought leader at a Fortune 500 technology corporation, managing one of the world's top 10 Hall-of-Fame training organizations.

As a prolific author of 50 multi-genre books, Dr. Attri writes books and articles on various topics ranging from business and leadership to performance and expertise, as well as training and development to HR and workforce development.

Passionate about continuous learning, Dr. Attri has earned two doctorates in learning, over 100 international educational credentials, several degrees and diplomas, and some of the highest certifications. He is an authentic accelerated learning business coach who practices what he preaches.

Featured in over 125 articles, interviews, and shows, Dr. Attri was awarded as one of the Most Admired Global Indians of 2022. He is a highly sought-after expert whose remarkable achievements continue to inspire everyone he touches to strive for true excellence in their personal and professional lives.

CONTENTS

1
TRAINING EVALUATION CHALLENGE

Training Effectiveness, Impact and ROI	- 3 -
Measuring TE vs ROI	- 7 -
Models for measurement	- 9 -
Why current models do not work	- 18 -
Challenges In Measurement	- 22 -
Making measurements easy	- 26 -

2
MEASURING LARGE-SCALE TECHNICAL TRAINING PROGRAMS

Large-scale training programs	- 33 -
Complex technical training programs	- 36 -
Why large-scale complex technical training programs	- 39 -
Measuring complex large-scale technical training programs	- 42 -
Making Measurement Simple for Managers	- 48 -

3
AN INTUITIVE MODEL FOR TECHNICAL TRAINING MANAGERS

A Common-Sense Model For Engineers	- 59 -
4-Tier Representation of ROE Model	- 62 -

4
DATA COLLECTION IN ROE MODEL

Data Collection	- 67 -
Step 1: Competency Map from Job Performance Metrics	- 71 -
Step 2: Pre-training baseline	- 74 -
Step 3: Post-Training Self-Assessment	- 80 -
Step 4: Post-Training Supervisor's Assessment	- 81 -

Step 5: Quarterly Job Performance — - 83 -
Step 6: Quarterly Business Performance Indicators — - 86 -

5
MEASURING REACTION INDEX

Why reaction index — - 91 -
The Process — - 92 -

6
MEASURING IMPROVEMENT INDEX

Why Improvement index — - 99 -
The Process — - 100 -

7
MEASURING EFFECTIVENESS INDEX

Why Effectiveness index — - 109 -
The Process — - 110 -

8
MEASURING IMPACT INDEX

Why Impact index — 119 —
The Process — 120 —

9
APPLYING THE MODEL IN PRACTICE

The Business — 127 —
Training ROI Challenge — 130 —
Step 1: Competency Map from Job Performance Metrics — 132 —
Step 2: Pre-training Baseline — 139 —
Step 3: Post-training assessment — 145 —
Step 4: Post-training Supervisor's assessment — 147 —
Step 5: Quarterly Job Performance — 151 —
Step 6: Quarterly Business Performance — 155 —
Recap — 156 —

10
FINAL THOUGHTS

11
CAREER ACCELERATION RESOURCES

Learn from power-packed books	- 167 -
Enroll in online training courses	- 169 -
Get certified in the science of speed	- 171 -
Insightful Keynotes For Your Events	- 172 -

1

TRAINING EVALUATION CHALLENGE

TRAINING IMPACT MEASUREMENT

TRAINING EFFECTIVENESS, IMPACT AND ROI

Training is an essential component of organizational development. Several businesses invest their significant resources in training programs to improve employee performance and productivity.

Training evaluation means how well the training program served an organization's goals if the dollar and time were well spent on it. According to James Kirkpatrick, a pioneer in training effectiveness measurement, "Evaluation is not an afterthought to training, but rather is meant to be integrated into the entire learning and development process" (2016).

There are three terms typically used interchangeably by leaders to connote training evaluation, although they represent distinct concepts: training effectiveness (TE), training impact (TI), and training return on investment (TROI)), as shown in Figure 1.

This section aims to clarify and qualify each of these terms. In the remainder of this book, these terms will be used interchangeably to mean the impact of training programs.

Figure 1: Training evaluation terms

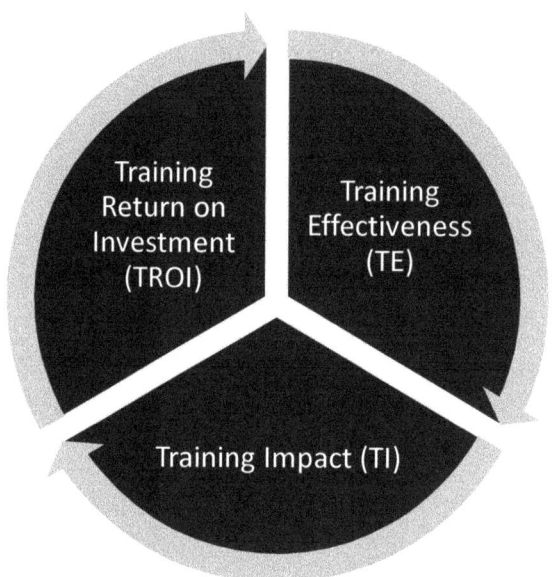

Training Effectiveness (TE)

Training effectiveness (TE) is the degree to which a training program achieves its intended outcomes. It refers to the extent to which a training program enables learners to acquire knowledge, skills, and attitudes relevant to their work and contribute to achieving organizational goals. Evaluating TE is essential for ensuring that training programs are meeting their objectives and delivering value to the organization.

TRAINING IMPACT MEASUREMENT

TE can be viewed in different ways depending on the perspective of the stakeholders involved. For instance, trainers and instructional designers may view effectiveness in terms of whether a training program meets its learning objectives and engages learners or not. Managers may view effectiveness in terms of whether a training program improves performance and productivity. Learners may view effectiveness in terms of whether the training program is relevant to their job and enhances their skills and knowledge.

Effective training ensures that employees can apply their learning on the job and improve their performance. For example, a retail organization may conduct a training program to improve its customer service. This program's effectiveness can be measured by assessing how well the employees apply the learned customer service skills while interacting with customers. The improved customer satisfaction levels indicate that the training program was very effective.

Training impact

Training impact, on the other hand, refers to the broader effects of training on an organization. It is a measure of the extent to which training contributes in the achievement of business objectives. Impact evaluation assesses the organizational benefits that result from training, such as increased revenue, reduced costs, or improved customer satisfaction.

For instance, a manufacturing organization may conduct a training program to improve the quality of its products. The impact of training can be measured by assessing whether the product quality improved after the training program. If training led to a reduction in product defects and customer complaints, it indicates that it had a positive impact on the organization.

Return on Investment (ROI)

Return on investment (ROI) is a financial metric evaluation that measures the ratio of the financial benefits of training to its costs. It is a measure of the effectiveness and impact of training in financial terms.

For example, a healthcare organization may conduct a training program to reduce patient readmissions. The ROI of training can be measured by comparing its cost to the financial benefits resulting from reduced readmissions. If the cost of training is less than the savings resulting from the reduced readmissions, it indicates a positive ROI.

TRAINING IMPACT MEASUREMENT

Although the terms TE, TI, and TROI are related, they are distinct concepts that require different evaluation methods. TE can be evaluated through methods such as pre- and post-training assessments, skills tests, and supervisor ratings. Impact evaluation requires the measurement of organizational metrics, such as productivity, revenue, and customer satisfaction, before and after training. ROI evaluation requires the comparison of the financial benefits of training to its costs.

Irrespective of similarity and distinction, measuring the effectiveness, impact, and ROI of training is critical for organizations to assess the value of their training programs. It requires a well-designed evaluation plan that considers the unique needs of an organization and its employees. By appropriate measurements, organizations can make data-driven decisions to improve their employee performance, organizational effectiveness, and financial performance.

MEASURING TE VS ROI

As a training leader, it is important that you do not get confused between measuring TE and TROI. Measuring TROI and TE are both important aspects of evaluating the impact of training programs, but they differ in their focus and methods. TE measurement focuses on assessing the outcomes of training program in terms of learners' acquisition of knowledge, skills, and attitudes relevant to their work, while training ROI measurement focuses on the financial impact of a training program.

TE measurement focuses on assessing the degree to which a training program meets its intended goals and objectives. Thus, the primary focus is on assessing the outcomes of the training program in terms of learners' acquisition of knowledge, skills, and attitudes that are relevant to their work and contribute to the achievement of organizational goals. Evaluation methods for TE can include pre- and post-training assessments, surveys, observations, and feedback from learners and stakeholders. The results of this evaluation are used to identify areas where the training program was successful and areas where improvement is needed.

In contrast, measuring training ROI involves calculating the financial return on investment from a training program. The primary focus is on assessing the economic impact of training program in terms of its costs and benefits. This can include factors such as the cost of training program, the time and resources required to deliver the program, and the impact of program on organizational outcomes such as productivity, revenue, and cost savings. Evaluation methods for training ROI can include cost-benefit analysis, cost-effectiveness analysis, and return-on-investment analysis. The results of this evaluation are used to demonstrate the financial value of training program to the stakeholders.

TRAINING IMPACT MEASUREMENT

The methods or approaches used to measure TE and TROI have some similarities as well as contrasts. Measuring TE provides information on the degree to which a training program meets its intended goals and objectives. On the other hand, measuring TROI provides information on the financial impact of the training program.

Both of these approaches have certain limitations as they rely on certain methods that may not fully capture the complex and multifaceted nature of training programs and their impact on organizational outcomes. Additionally, both approaches may be affected by factors outside the control of training programs, such as changes in the economy, technological advances, or shifts in organizational strategy.

Therefore, it is important to use a range of evaluation methods to interpret the results in the context of a broader organizational environment. By combining these two approaches, organizations can gain a more comprehensive understanding of the impact of their training programs on both learning outcomes and organizational outcomes.

MODELS FOR MEASUREMENT

There are several models and frameworks that can be used to measure TE, TIt, and TROI. In this response, I will discuss some of the most famous models and frameworks, including Kirkpatrick's Four-Level Model, Phillips' Five-

Level Model, Brinkerhoff's Success Case Method, and the CIPP Model. I will also explain how these models and frameworks address each other's limitations.

Kirkpatrick's Four-Level Model

Kirkpatrick's Four-Level Model is one of the most widely used models for evaluating TE. This model includes four levels of evaluation, as summarized in Table 1.

Table 1: Kirkpatrick's 4-level model

Level	Intent	Meaning
Level 1	Reaction	Measures learners' reaction to the training program
Level 2	Learning	Measures the extent to which learners acquired knowledge, skills, and attitudes during a training program
Level 3	Behavior	Measures the extent to which learners apply what they learned during the training program on the job
Level 4	Results (impact)	Measures the impact of training program on organizational outcomes such as productivity, revenue, and cost savings

TRAINING IMPACT MEASUREMENT

Figure 2 graphically represents these four levels. A typical representation is a pyramid where the Reaction is at the base or the first level while the top shows measures related to Results.

One of the limitations of Kirkpatrick's Four-Level Model is that it does not provide guidance on how to identify the specific outcomes that should be measured at each level. Additionally, the model does not consider other factors that may be influencing organizational outcomes.

Figure 2: Kirkpatrick 4-level training evaluation model

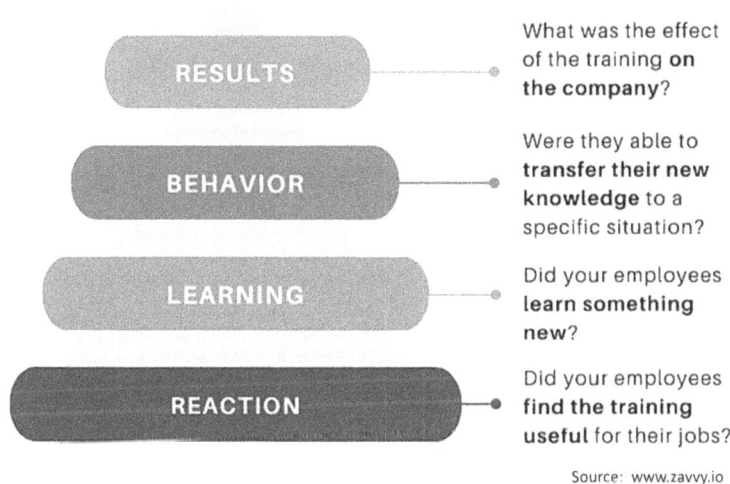

Source: www.zavvy.io

Phillips' Five-Level Model

Phillips' Five-Level Model is an extension of Kirkpatrick's Model, which includes a fifth level, ROI, as summarized in Table 2 and Figure 3.

Table 2: Phillips' 5-level model

Level	Intent	Meaning
Level 1	Reaction	Measures learners' reaction to the training program
Level 2	Learning	Measures the extent to which learners acquired knowledge, skills, and attitudes during the training program
Level 3	Behavior	Measures the extent to which learners apply what they learned during the training program on the job
Level 4	Results (impact)	Measures the impact of training programs on organizational outcomes such as productivity, revenue, and cost savings
Level 5	ROI	Measures the financial return on investment from the training program

While the previous four levels have the exact same intent as Kirkpatrick, the fifth level measures the financial ROI

TRAINING IMPACT MEASUREMENT

from the training program and is particularly useful for demonstrating the value of training to stakeholders.

Figure 3 shows Phillip's ROI model in the form of a pyramid in which the ROI tier is at the apex of the pyramid.

One of the limitations of Phillips' Five-Level Model is that it can be difficult to calculate the financial impact of a training program accurately. Additionally, the model does not guide how to identify the specific outcomes that should be measured at each level.

Figure 3: Phillip's five-level ROI model

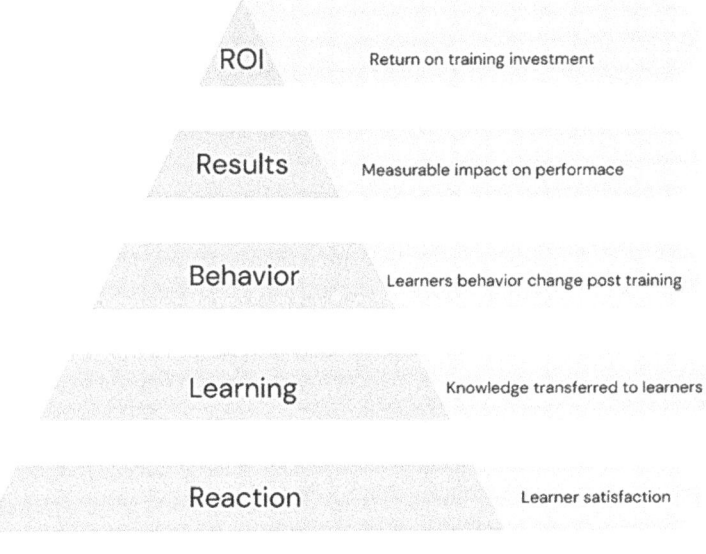

CH 1 - TRAINING EVALUATION CHALLENGE

Brinkerhoff's Success Case Method

Brinkerhoff's Success Case Method is a qualitative approach to evaluating TE. As shown in Figure 4, this method involves five steps to identify successful and unsuccessful learners and conduct in-depth interviews to understand the factors that contributed to their success or failure.

Figure 4: Brokerhoff's success case method

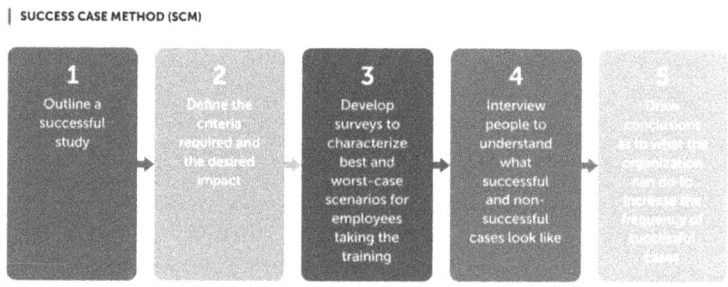

One of its limitations is that it can be time-consuming and may not provide a comprehensive understanding of training program's impact on organizational outcomes.

Learning transfer evaluation model (LTEM)

LTEM is a multi-tiered method for evaluating TE. It combines learning with the transfer of new skills into workplace processes. This model, as shown in Figure 5,

TRAINING IMPACT MEASUREMENT

examines multiple factors that make up the whole learning experience.

Figure 5: Learning transfer evaluation model

LEARNING-TRANSFER EVALUATION MODEL (LTEM)

1. **Attendance** — signing up for the course
2. **Activity** — participant's interest and attention
3. **Learner Perceptions** — their motivation to apply the knowledge
4. **Knowledge** — the expertise imparted
5. **Decision-making Competence** — utilizing knowledge within realistic scenarios
6. **Task Competence** — remembering relevant knowledge or skills for a given situation
7. **Transfer** — applying knowledge either with assistance or independently
8. **Effects of Transfer** — evaluating the impact of knowledge transfer

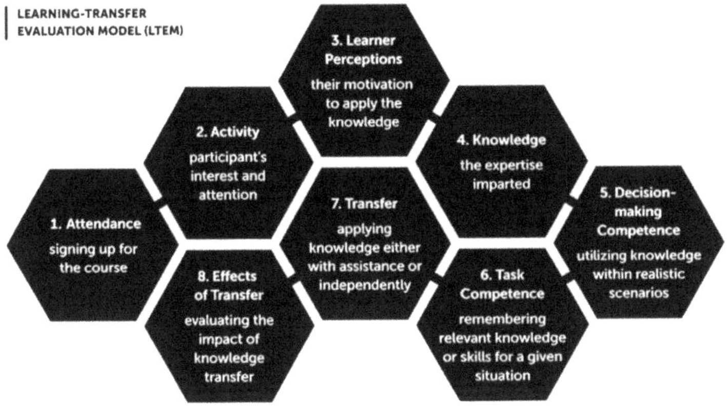

Source: valamis.com

It consists of eight levels, as summarized in Table 3.

Table 3: LTEM 8-level model

Level	Intent	Meaning
Level 1	Attendance	Signing up for the course
Level 2	Activity	Participant's interest and attention
Level 3	Learner Perceptions	Their motivation to apply the knowledge

Level 4	Knowledge	The expertise imparted
Level 5	Decision-making Competence	Utilizing knowledge within realistic scenarios
Level 6	Task Competence	Remembering relevant knowledge or skills for a given situation
Level 7	Transfer	Applying knowledge either with assistance or independently
Level 8	Effects of Transfer	Evaluating the impact of knowledge transfer

CIPP Model

The CIPP Model (Context, Input, Process, Product), as shown in Figure 6, is a comprehensive framework for evaluating TE.

This model includes four components, as summarized in Table 4. One of the strengths of the CIPP Model is that it provides a comprehensive framework for evaluating TE. However, the model can be complex and require significant resources.

TRAINING IMPACT MEASUREMENT

Table 4: CIPP 4-component model

Component	Intent	Meaning
1	Context	The context in which a training program is implemented
2	Input	The resources and materials used in training program
3	Process	The delivery of training program
4	Product	The outcomes of the training program

Figure 6: Context, Input, Process, Product model

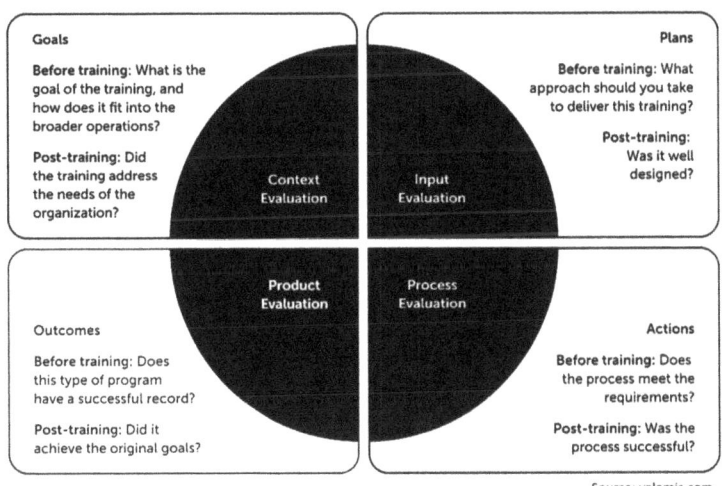

Source: valamis.com

CH 1 - TRAINING EVALUATION CHALLENGE

Using Models based on context

To address the limitations of these models and frameworks, organizations can combine different models and approaches to gain a more comprehensive understanding of their training programs' impact. For example, Kirkpatrick's Four-Level Model and Phillips' Five-Level Model can be combined to assess the effectiveness and ROI of a training program.

Similarly, Brinkerhoff's Success Case Method can be used in conjunction with other models to provide a more in-depth understanding of the factors that contribute to training success or failure. The CIPP Model can be used to provide a comprehensive evaluation of the training program that considers contextual factors, input, process, and product. By using appropriate measures and evaluation models, organizations can gain valuable insights into the impact of training and make an informed decision.

WHY CURRENT MODELS DO NOT WORK

Current training effectiveness, impact, and ROI (TE/TI/TROI) models have limitations that can make it difficult to measure the impact of training programs accurately. Some of the key reasons why traditional models fail are discussed here:

TRAINING IMPACT MEASUREMENT

Over-reliance on Quantitative Measures

Many current TE/TI/TROI models rely on quantitative measures such as surveys and tests to evaluate the impact of training programs. While quantitative measures can be useful in assessing learning outcomes, they may not capture the full range of outcomes that are important to stakeholders.

For example, if the goal of a training program is to improve employee engagement, a survey may be an appropriate measure to assess changes in employee satisfaction with their work. However, it may not capture more subjective factors, such as changes in employee motivation or commitment to the organization.

Failure to consider contextual factors

Current TE/TI/TROI models often fail to consider contextual factors that may influence the impact of training programs. Contextual factors can include organizational culture, leadership support, and external factors such as economic conditions and regulatory changes.

For example, if a training program is implemented during a period of significant organizational change, it may be difficult to isolate the effects of training program from other factors that are influencing employee performance.

Lack of consideration for individual differences

Current models for TE/TI/TROI measurements often do not consider individual differences among learners that may influence the impact of training programs. Individual differences can include factors such as prior knowledge, motivation, and learning style.

For example, if a training program is designed for a diverse group of learners with different learning styles and preferences, a one-size-fits-all approach may not be effective in meeting the needs of all learners.

Focus on short-term outcomes

Many current models for TE/TI/TROI measurements focus on short-term outcomes, such as changes in knowledge or skills immediately following a training program. While short-term outcomes can be important indicators of the effectiveness of a training program, they may not capture the longer-term impact of program on the organizational outcomes.

TRAINING IMPACT MEASUREMENT

For example, if a training program is designed to improve employee retention rates, changes in retention rates may not be evident immediately following the training program but may become evident over time as employees apply what they learned on the job.

Failure to measure the intangible benefits of training

Current models for TE/TI/TROI measurements often fail to measure the intangible benefits of training, such as improvements in organizational culture or changes in employee attitudes and values. These intangible benefits may be difficult to quantify, but they have a significant impact on organizational outcomes.

For example, if a training program is designed to improve employee engagement, changes in employee attitudes and values may be important indicators of the effectiveness of program, but may be difficult to measure using traditional quantitative measures.

The limitations in current TE/TI/TROI models make it difficult to measure the impact of training programs accurately. To address these limitations, organizations can use a variety of measures and evaluation models that consider the full range of outcomes that are important to stakeholders. Additionally, organizations can take a more holistic approach to measure the impact of training programs, which includes a consideration of contextual factors, individual differences, and the intangible benefits of training.

CHALLENGES IN MEASUREMENT

Measuring TE/TI/TROI is a complex process that presents several challenges, as summarized in Figure 7.

These challenges can make it difficult for organizations to accurately assess the impact of training programs and make informed decisions about how to improve them.

For example, if the goal of a training program is to improve customer service skills, a survey may be an appropriate measure to assess customer satisfaction with the service provided by trained employees. However, if the goal of training program is to improve the accuracy and efficiency of data entry, a performance assessment may be a more appropriate measure to assess the number of errors made before and after the training program.

TRAINING IMPACT MEASUREMENT

Figure 7: Challenges in TE measurements

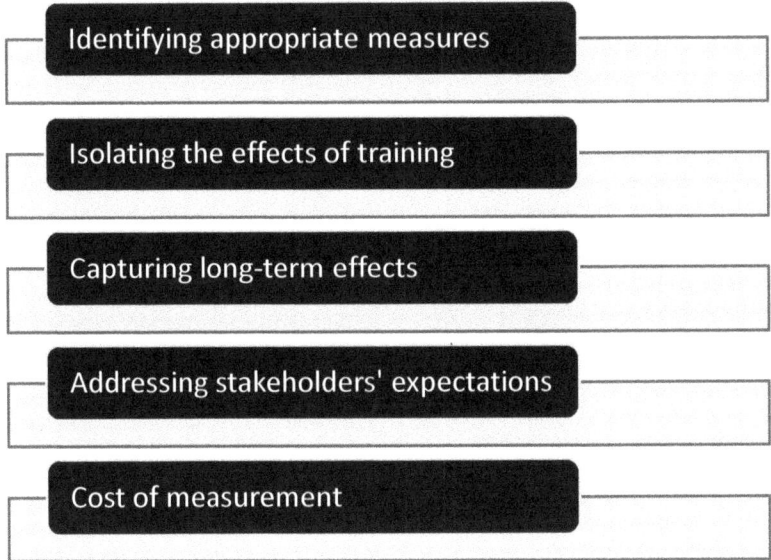

Isolating the effects of training

Another challenge in measuring TE/TI/TROI is isolating the effects of training from other factors that may be influencing performance. While assessing whether a learner has acquired knowledge or demonstrated skill may be relatively straightforward, it can be more difficult to determine how much this learning has translated into improved performance and productivity. This is particularly true for complex or multifaceted training programs where it may be challenging to isolate the effects of training from other factors that

CH 1 - TRAINING EVALUATION CHALLENGE

may be influencing performance. For example, if an organization is implementing a new software system at the same time as a training program, it may be difficult to determine the extent to which improvements in performance are due to the training program or new software system.

One way to address this challenge is to use a control group that does not receive training to compare with the group that receives training. This can help to isolate the effects of training program from other factors influencing the performance.

Capturing long-term effects

Measuring the long-term effects of training can also present a challenge. While it may be relatively easy to measure short-term improvements in performance immediately following a training program, it can be more difficult to determine the extent to which these improvements are sustained over time.

For example, if a training program is designed to improve sales skills, it may be easy to measure short-term improvements in sales performance immediately following the training program. However, it may be more difficult to determine the extent to which these improvements are sustained over a longer period of time, such as six months or a year after the training program.

Addressing stakeholders' expectations

Stakeholders' expectations can also present a challenge in measuring TE, impact, and ROI. Different stakeholders may have different expectations for what a training program should achieve, and these expectations may be difficult to reconcile.

For example, if a training program aims to improve employee engagement and job satisfaction, managers may expect to see an improvement in employee retention rates after this. However, employees may have altogether different expectations, such as improved work-life balance or greater opportunities for career development.

Cost of measurement

Measuring TE/TI/TROI often requires collecting and analyzing data, which can be time-consuming and expensive. So, another challenge here is the cost of measurement.

For example, if an organization is conducting a return-on-investment analysis to assess the

CH 1 - TRAINING EVALUATION CHALLENGE

financial impact of a training program, it may need to collect data on the cost of training program, the time and resources required to deliver that program, and its impact on the organizational outcomes such as productivity, revenue, and cost savings. Collecting and analyzing this data can be expensive and time-consuming.

Thus, as we see, measuring TE/TI/TROI presents several challenges that can make it difficult for organizations to assess the impact of their training programs accurately. Despite these challenges, it is essential for organizations to evaluate the TE in order to ensure that they are meeting their objectives and delivering value to the organization. In the end, effective training can improve employee performance and productivity, increase job satisfaction and retention, and contribute to the achievement of organizational goals. In contrast, ineffective training can result in wasted resources and decreased employee morale.

MAKING MEASUREMENTS EASY

To overcome these challenges, organizations can take several steps, such as:

Defining clear goals and objectives: Before implementing a training program, it is essential to define clear goals and objectives. This will help organizations to select appropriate measures, evaluate the effectiveness of program, and assess its impact on organizational outcomes.

Choosing appropriate measures: Organizations should choose appropriate measures to assess the outcomes of training. This may involve using different measures for different types of training and learning outcomes.

Using a control group: To isolate the effects of training from other factors that may be influencing performance, organizations can use a control group that does not receive training.

Capturing long-term effects: To capture the long-term effects of training, organizations can conduct follow-up assessments at regular intervals after the training program.

Communicating with stakeholders: Organizations should communicate with stakeholders to understand their expectations for a training program and to ensure that they are aware of its goals and objectives.

Conducting cost-benefit analysis: To determine the cost-effectiveness of a training program, organizations can conduct a cost-benefit analysis to assess the financial impact of the program.

2
MEASURING LARGE-SCALE TECHNICAL TRAINING PROGRAMS

TRAINING IMPACT MEASUREMENT

Organizations are becoming larger in scope and business operations. Hence, their training programs are becoming large-scale, spanning countries, product portfolios, employee bases, and investments. Most organizations are now technology-savvy. That leads them to institute complex product training and technical training programs, which are usually quite intense. Measuring such large-scale, complex training programs' effectiveness, impact, and ROI is difficult. I will explain this by splitting the problem between large-scale training programs and complex technical training programs.

In a nutshell, 10 challenges make it daunting to measure TE, as shown in Figure 8.

Figure 8: Challenges in TE measurements for large-scale, complex technical training programs

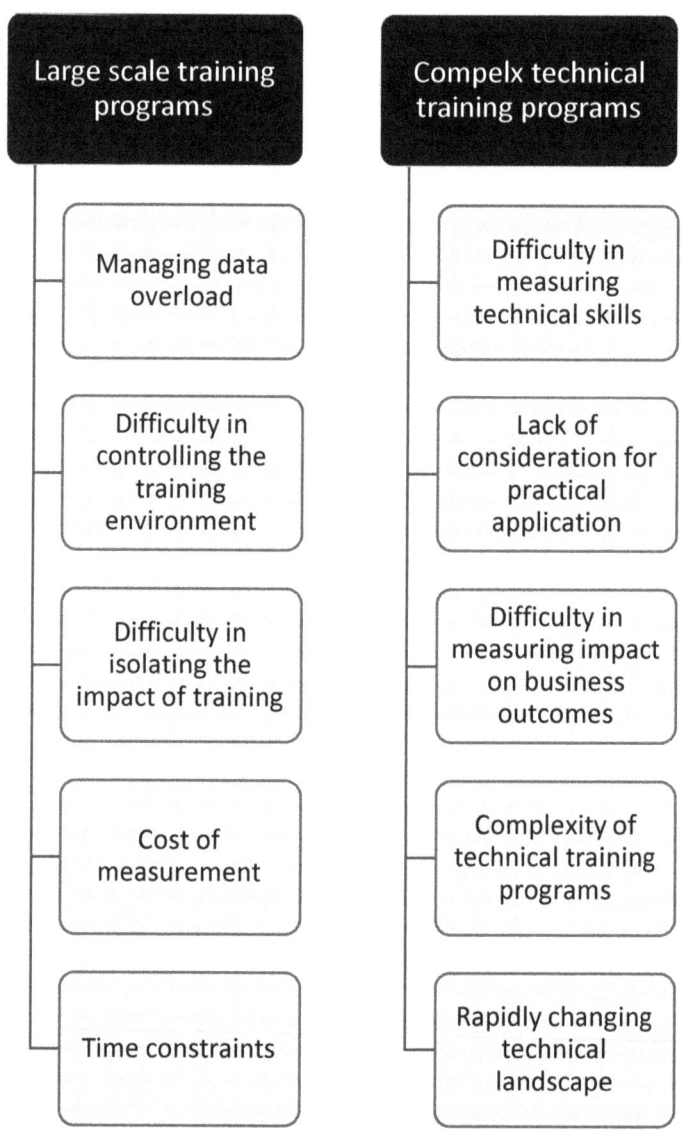

TRAINING IMPACT MEASUREMENT

LARGE-SCALE TRAINING PROGRAMS

Measuring TE is critical to determine whether training programs are meeting their intended goals and producing the desired outcomes. However, current TE measurement models can face significant challenges when applied to large-scale training programs.

Managing data overload

Large-scale training programs involve a considerable amount of data, making it difficult to manage and analyze. Training evaluation models that rely on collecting data through surveys, assessments, and interviews can create a data overload, leading to a significant amount of data that needs to be managed and analyzed. The sheer volume of data generated by a large-scale training program can make it difficult to identify and prioritize key metrics, interpret the results and gain actionable insights.

According to O'Reilly and Farndale (2013), large organizations may face issues with data management, such as collecting data from multiple sources, data accuracy and integrity, and analyzing data to identify patterns and trends. These issues can make it challenging to develop great TE/TI/TROI measurement models for large-scale training programs.

Difficulty in controlling the training environment

Large-scale training programs often take place in different locations, making it challenging to control the training environment. Participants may attend training in different geographical locations or attend training online, which can lead to a lack of consistency in training delivery and assessment methods.

Additionally, large-scale training programs may involve different trainers and training providers, leading to variations in training delivery and assessment quality. According to Leimbach (2017), the lack of consistency in training delivery and assessment can create challenges in developing and implementing effectiveness measurement models for large-scale training programs.

Difficulty in isolating the impact of training

Large-scale training programs can make it challenging to isolate the impact of training from other factors that may be influencing employee performance. Other factors, such as changes in the economy, new technology, or new products, can also affect employee performance, making it difficult to determine the true impact of training programs.

According to Noe (2017), to isolate the impact of training, organizations need to use control groups that

TRAINING IMPACT MEASUREMENT

do not receive training to compare their performance with the performance of employees who receive training. However, it may be impossible to create control groups in large-scale training programs due to logistical constraints or resource limitations.

Cost of measurement

Measuring TE of large-scale training programs can be costly as they involve a large number of participants. The cost of data collection, analysis, and reporting can be high, making it difficult for organizations to allocate resources to measure TE.

According to Jolivette and Woo (2018), the cost of measurement can be particularly high for large-scale training programs, which may require a significant investment in resources to collect and analyze data. Organizations may face challenges in justifying the cost of measurement and may not allocate sufficient resources to measure TE accurately.

Time constraints

Large-scale training programs may be time-constrained, making it difficult to implement comprehensive TE/TI/TROI measurement models. According to Leimbach (2017), large-scale training programs may require quick and efficient data collection and analysis methods to provide timely feedback to stakeholders.

TE/TI/TROI measurement models that require a lengthy and time-consuming evaluation process may not be practical for large-scale training programs. Organizations may need to consider using more agile and flexible evaluation methods that can quickly provide actionable insights into the effectiveness of training programs.

COMPLEX TECHNICAL TRAINING PROGRAMS

Technical training is a critical aspect of workforce development, particularly in the manufacturing, healthcare, and information technology industries. Technical training programs are designed to provide employees with the knowledge, skills, and competencies required to perform their tasks effectively. However, measuring the effectiveness of such programs can be challenging, as traditional TE/TI/TROI models may fail to capture their unique features and outcomes.

Difficulty in measuring technical skills

Technical training programs focus on developing technical skills, which can be challenging to measure using traditional TE/TI/TROI measurement models. Traditional models often rely on subjective measures, such as self-reported surveys and assessments, which may not provide an accurate picture of technical proficiency. Moreover, they may also fail to capture the practical demonstration of technical skills and knowledge.

According to Golaszewski and Biddle (2012), measuring technical TE requires a more comprehensive approach that includes both subjective and objective measures. Objective measures can include performance assessments and practical demonstrations of skills, while subjective measures can include surveys and self-assessments.

Lack of consideration for practical application

Technical training programs focus on developing skills that can be applied in a practical setting. Traditional TE/TI/TROI measurement models may fail to capture the practical application of skills by focusing too heavily on theoretical knowledge. Technical skills are best learned through hands-on experience, which may not be adequately captured by traditional models.

According to Jaap and Duckworth (2014), technical TE/TI/TROI measurement models need to consider the practical application of skills and competencies; which can be evaluated through observation, performance assessments, and simulations.

CH 2 - MEASURING LARGE SCALE TECHNICAL TRAINING

Difficulty in measuring impact on business

Technical training programs are designed to improve technical skills and competencies, which may not directly translate to business outcomes. Traditional TE models may fail to capture the impact of technical training on business outcomes, such as productivity, efficiency, and profitability.

According to Pohlandt-McCormick and Kazanas (2019), technical TE/TI/TROI measurement models need to consider the impact of training on business outcomes to provide a comprehensive picture. This evaluation requires a robust evaluation model that considers the unique factors contributing to business success.

The complexity of technical training programs

Technical training programs can be complex and involve multiple learning objectives and outcomes. Traditional TE/TI/TROI measurement models may fail to capture the full range of outcomes and may focus too heavily on specific learning objectives.

According to Stolovitch and Keeps (2011), technical TE models need to consider the complexity of technical training programs and their multiple learning objectives and outcomes. Thus, evaluation models need to be tailored to the unique needs of technical training

TRAINING IMPACT MEASUREMENT

programs. This requires incorporating a range of measures to capture the full range of outcomes.

Rapidly changing technical landscape

Technical training programs need to keep up with the rapidly changing technical landscape, which can make it difficult for traditional training models to evaluate their effectiveness over time and capture the changing nature of technical skills and competencies.

According to Chen and Pan (2013), technicalTE/TI/TROI measurement models need to consider the rapidly changing technical landscape and incorporate measures to capture the adaptability and flexibility of technical training programs.

WHY LARGE-SCALE COMPLEX TECHNICAL TRAINING PROGRAMS

In the modern era, businesses need to constantly adapt to the fast-paced changes in technology and market dynamics. This requires them to stay ahead of the competition by investing in their employees through highly competitive technical training programs.

Almost all businesses currently employ technical training programs which are continually becoming complex and large-

CH 2 - MEASURING LARGE SCALE TECHNICAL TRAINING

scale. These programs can cover a wide range of topics, from technical skills, such as software development, data analytics, and cybersecurity, to non-technical skills, such as leadership, project management, and communication.

These training programs can take many forms, including in-person classroom training, virtual instructor-led training, self-paced online courses, and on-the-job training. They can also involve various delivery methods, such as lectures, simulations, case studies, and hands-on exercises.

To stay competitive:

In today's global marketplace, businesses need to stay ahead of the competition by ensuring that their employees have the latest technical knowledge and skills. This can only be achieved through regular training programs, which can improve their employees' performance. Well-trained employees are more confident, competent, and capable of handling new challenges.

For instance, imagine a software development company that relies on a particular programming language. If the company fails to keep up with the latest trends and advancements in that language, it risks losing its competitive edge. By investing in complex, large-scale technical training programs, the company can ensure

TRAINING IMPACT MEASUREMENT

that its employees are always up to date on the latest developments.

To increase employee retention:

Employees are more likely to stay with a company that invests in their growth and development. By offering complex, large-scale technical training programs, businesses can show their employees that they value them and are committed to helping them grow in their careers. Employees who receive training are more likely to be satisfied with their jobs because it provides them with opportunities for growth and development, which can lead to higher levels of job satisfaction.

Moreover, offering training programs can help businesses attract new talent. When job seekers see that a company is committed to investing in its employees, they are more likely to be attracted to that company.

To improve efficiency and productivity:

By improving their employees' skills, businesses can increase efficiency and productivity. Well-trained employees are more confident and capable of performing their jobs, resulting in higher quality work and faster turnaround times.

For instance, consider a manufacturing company that invests in a training program that teaches employees how to use new machinery. By providing this training, the company can ensure that its employees are using the machinery correctly and safely. This, in turn, can result in fewer accidents, less downtime, and increased production.

To meet regulatory requirements:

Many industries have specific regulations and standards that businesses must comply with. This can include regulations related to data privacy, cybersecurity, and workplace safety.

Businesses can ensure that their employees know and follow these regulations by offering complex, large-scale technical training programs. This can help them to avoid costly penalties and legal issues.

MEASURING COMPLEX LARGE-SCALE TECHNICAL TRAINING PROGRAMS

As we see, applying current TE/TI/TROI measurement models to large-scale training programs as well as complex technical training programs, can be challenging due to several factors.

TRAINING IMPACT MEASUREMENT

Some of the factors highlighted above are data overload, difficulty in controlling the training environment, difficulty in isolating the impact of training, cost of measurement, time constraints, the complexity of programs, and rapidly changing technical space etc.

Figure 9: Measuring training impact for complex, large-scale technical training programs

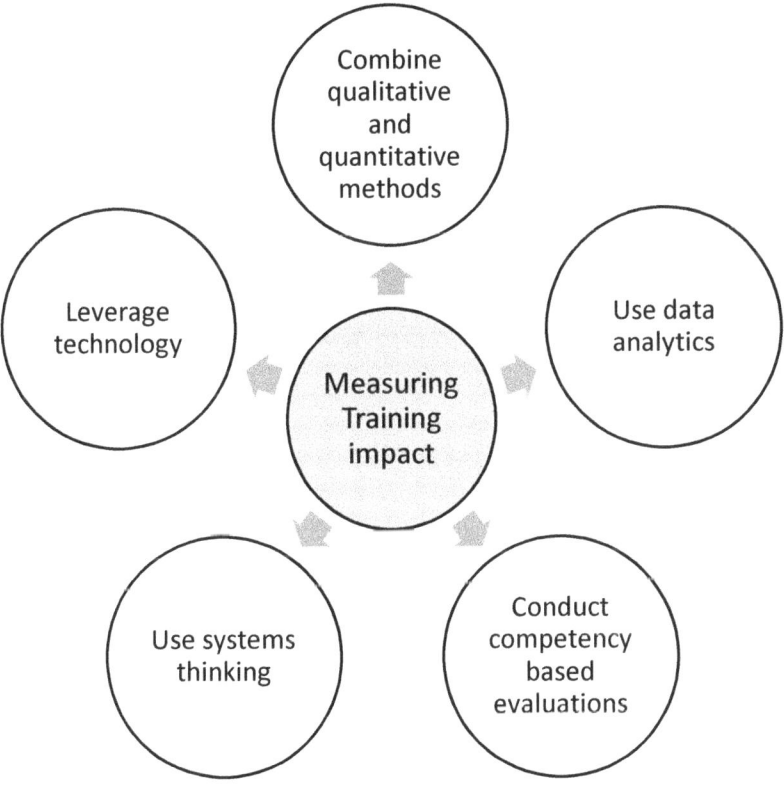

CH 2 - MEASURING LARGE SCALE TECHNICAL TRAINING

Therefore, organizations need to carefully consider these challenges and develop evaluation models that are tailored to their unique needs of large-scale, complex technical training programs.

Organizations need to incorporate a range of measures to capture the full range of outcomes. This can include a combination of subjective and objective measures, practical assessments, simulations, and evaluations of the impact on business outcomes. Additionally, they need to consider the rapidly changing technical landscape and incorporate measures accordingly.

At a high level, you need to follow five considerations to measure the impact of complex, large-scale, technical training programs, as shown in Figure 9.

Combining qualitative and quantitative methods

One approach to overcome these challenges is to use a combination of quantitative and qualitative measures. Organizations can leverage technology and data analytics to streamline data collection and analysis, reducing the cost and time required to measure TE.

One model that has been proposed for large-scale training programs is the Success Case Method (SCM) developed by Brinkerhoff (2003). SCM is a qualitative evaluation method that focuses on identifying successful training cases and analyzing the factors that contribute

TRAINING IMPACT MEASUREMENT

to success. This method involves identifying a sample of successful and unsuccessful trainees and conducting in-depth interviews to understand the factors that contributed to their success or failure.

SCM has several advantages for large-scale training programs. It is flexible and can be used to evaluate different types of training programs, including those involving many participants. Additionally, SCM is a cost-effective approach that does not require extensive resources or data collection.

Using data analytics

Another approach that has been proposed for large-scale training programs is to use data analytics and machine learning to analyze large data sets. This approach involves collecting data from various sources, including online assessments, surveys, and training records, and using data analytics and machine learning algorithms to identify patterns and trends in the data.

Data analytics can help organizations identify which training programs are most effective and which factors contribute to training success. Machine learning algorithms can be used to develop predictive models that can forecast the training's impact on organizational outcomes, such as employee turnover, productivity, and revenue.

One example of this approach is the work by Xie and Li (2017). They proposed a method that uses a deep neural network algorithm to predict the effectiveness of training programs. This method involves collecting data from various sources, including learner behavior, performance, and satisfaction.

Competency-based evaluation

Using a competency-based evaluation model is another approach to overcome the limitations of traditional TE/TI/TROI measurement models for technical training.

According to Muijtjens et al. (2013), competency-based evaluation models can provide a more comprehensive understanding of technical TE by evaluating the attainment of specific technical competencies rather than evaluating the overall effectiveness of training program. These models can include practical assessments and simulations to evaluate the practical application of technical skills and competencies.

Use systems thinking

Another approach to evaluate technical TE is to use a systems thinking approach. Systems thinking considers the complex interactions between the components of a system and how they contribute to its overall effectiveness.

According to Jackson et al. (2015), systems thinking can provide a more comprehensive understanding of technical TE by evaluating the interactions between technical skills, organizational processes, and business outcomes. It can help organizations identify the critical factors that contribute to technical TE and develop more targeted training programs.

Leverage technology

Organizations can leverage technology and data analytics to evaluate the effectiveness of technical training programs. Technology can be used to collect data from multiple sources, including online assessments, simulations, and performance metrics, and data analytics can be used to identify patterns and trends in the data.

According to Brinkman et al. (2017), technology and data analytics can provide a more comprehensive understanding of technical TE by capturing data from multiple sources and providing real-time feedback to stakeholders. Technology can also be used to develop adaptive training programs according to the changing technical landscape and provide more personalized training experiences.

CH 2 – MEASURING LARGE SCALE TECHNICAL TRAINING

In conclusion, current TE models face several challenges when applied to large-scale training programs. By applying various approaches, organizations can gain valuable insights into the effectiveness of technical training programs and make informed decisions about how to allocate resources to them.

MAKING MEASUREMENT SIMPLE FOR MANAGERS

Why Businesses need to defend the ROI of training

Modern businesses rely heavily on the technical training of their workforce. Take the example of a company selling and repairing complex hardware. They are tightly pressed to reduce the time-to-resolution to keep the profit margins as well as their customer satisfaction high. The skills of the workforce supporting such functions are critical to the organization.

Typically, complex troubleshooting and higher-order technical skills are affected through large-scale training programs. These are investment-intensive training programs that require money and resources. The substantial investments in training legitimately drive executives to ask: "**What is the ROI for a training program?**"

ROI is expressed by assigning dollar values to investments and tangible/non-tangible benefits. Measuring the worthiness of an investment using ROI and equivalent dollar value is a much-loved preference at the executive level because it gives a quantified figure which helps in making decisions quickly. Typically, executive staff and business managers are not training professionals, so they cannot relate well to a training program's soft or intangible benefits.

Therefore, they need training ROI as a crucial metric to show the overall business value of training. That is where the challenge comes. Typically, traditional training and learning managers are either not business managers or have a minimal finance background. They take years to develop such business acumen. Yet, they are still forced to do this and have little choice.

Why finding ROI is not a right approach

While the basic premise of ROI measurement to translate the value of training into dollars equivalent is very appealing, it is not always practical. The foremost challenge with the ROI approach is that it may take away the full perspective for which a training program is introduced in the first place – the skill gaps or skill enhancement. Admittedly, the skill gap must have some business or financial implications that could lead to the development or implementation of a training program under question.

The biggest argument given against the ROI measurement approach is that training and learning is a multi-dimensional process whose value cannot be articulated simply in dollars. Though the role of training in improving performance is well understood, researchers argue that performance during a training event is short-lived.

In a study, Bjork (2009, p. 313) expressed that performance during a training event may not be the right indicator: "Performance during training is often an unreliable guide to whether the desired learning has actually happened. Considerable learning can happen across periods when performance is not improving and, conversely, little or no learning can happen across periods when performance is improving markedly."

However, what matters is the job performance of an individual after training. Bjork (2009, p. 319) highlights a challenge as: "The problem for a training organization is to maximise performance when it matters, that is, after training and, specially, when individuals are deployed."

Similarly, Sonnentag and Frese (2002, p. 6) suggested: "One might argue that what ultimately counts for an organisation is the individuals' performance and not their learning—although learning might help to perform well. This line of reasoning stresses that learning is a highly relevant predictor of performance but is not performance itself." During any training intervention, learning is more important than in-training performance, while after training, on-the-job performance is more important than learning.

The real effectiveness of training or learning is the performance someone displays in the field. However, performance in a job role cannot be attributed only to a training program. Instead, it is attained through collective learning from several sources. Any training program does not work in isolation to produce outcomes or impacts during the actual job.

The outcomes and final job performance in a job role are attained through close interactions with other support functions like the manager's involvement, performance support systems, on-the-job mentoring, and on-demand continuous learning that happens after a training program. Thus, the ROI of a training program alone provides little to no context for true effect and true contributors toward the performance.

Therefore, evaluating training interventions involves many factors, including a measure of learning transfer and organizational impact. The complexity comes because of the dynamic interrelationship of organizational goals, business goals, training objectives, the profile of trainees, training situations, instructional technologies, and job environment. In complex training, the dynamics and factors that affect the outcome may be hard to isolate as the sole effect of training per se.

Traditional ROI Measurements are cumbersome

Business managers often struggle to explain the impact and ROI of their training programs, which can create challenges in securing funding for future training initiatives. One of the main reasons for this struggle is the complexity and lack of

CH 2 - MEASURING LARGE SCALE TECHNICAL TRAINING

practicality of existing TE/TI/TROI measurement models. These models fail to consider the unique needs and requirements of different businesses and industries, making it difficult to apply them to large-scale training programs effectively.

Current models often prioritize the financial aspect of training programs, such as ROI, over the actual effectiveness of training in improving employee performance and achieving business goals. This focus on financial outcomes may not accurately reflect the true value of training as other factors, such as employee engagement and job satisfaction. are also important indicators of TE.

One of the reasons why business managers find it difficult to explain the impact and ROI of their training programs is a lack of clarity on their training objectives. According to Noe (2017), organizations need to develop clear training objectives aligned with organizational goals and objectives. Clear training objectives can provide a framework for evaluating the effectiveness of training program and demonstrate its impact on organizational outcomes.

Another reason why business managers may face difficulty in explaining their training program's effectiveness is that it can be challenging to isolate the impact of training from other factors influencing the organizational outcomes. According to Kirkpatrick and Kirkpatrick (2016), evaluating the impact of training requires a comparison group that has not received the training. However, in many cases, it can be challenging to

TRAINING IMPACT MEASUREMENT

identify such a suitable comparison or control group that has not received the training.

Traditional TE/TI/TROI measurement models are often too complex and require extensive data collection and analysis, which can be time-consuming and costly. They may also fail to capture the specific outcomes and impact of technical training programs, which are typically more focused on skill-building and knowledge development than on overall business performance. This can lead to challenges in demonstrating the value of technical training programs to upper management and other stakeholders. According to Jolivette and Woo (2018), organizations need to develop a data collection and analysis plan that considers the unique needs of a training program. This can include using a combination of quantitative and qualitative measures and leveraging technology and data analytics.

Many business managers use traditional TE/TI/TROI measurement models, such as the Kirkpatrick model, which may not provide a comprehensive evaluation framework for measuring the impact and ROI of training programs. Sometimes Kirkpatrick's Training evaluation model and Phillips' ROI models, though widely used, turn too abstract to apply for technical and even engineering managers.

Traditional models often focus on short-term outcomes, such as knowledge and skill acquisition, and may not capture the longer-term impact of training on organizational outcomes. According to O'Reilly (2017), organizations need to develop a

CH 2 - MEASURING LARGE SCALE TECHNICAL TRAINING

comprehensive evaluation framework that considers the full range of outcomes, including the impact of training on business outcomes, such as productivity, efficiency, and revenue.

Thus, beyond doubt, measuring TE in a complex environment cannot effectively use the traditional methodologies of computer dollar-based ROI. It requires a different approach than modeling factors with a dollar equivalent for ROI computation.

Making measurement simple for business managers

To address these challenges, simpler and more practical TE/TI/TROI measurement frameworks are needed to be tailored to the unique needs and requirements of different businesses and industries.

Such a framework should be easy to use, cost-effective, and provide a comprehensive understanding of TE.

Given how such programs are typically structured in large organizations, I found leveraging feedback-based mechanisms to measure training program effectiveness much easier. The standard project management model and stakeholder management processes already leverage mechanisms of recurring feedback at multiple levels, which are more robust in technical training programs.

TRAINING IMPACT MEASUREMENT

Measure Return on expectations instead of Return on investment

There is a shift in methodology needed in the current business context to make it easy for business managers with a non-training background to measure the impact of training programs effortlessly. This shift is from financial-driven 'return on investment' to comparison-driven 'return on expectations,' as shown in Figure 10.

Figure 10: Shift in training impact methodology

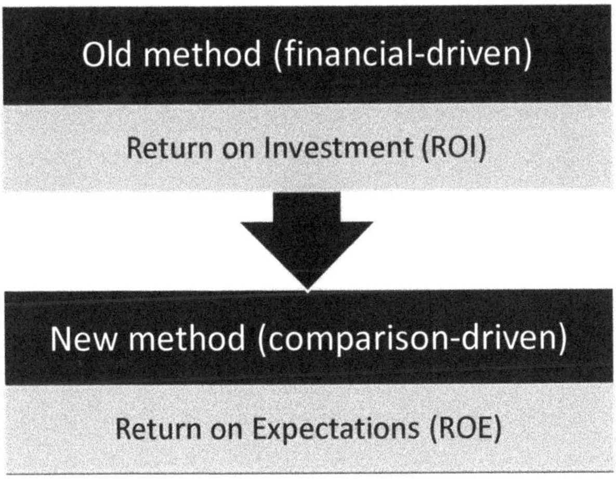

```
┌─────────────────────────────────────────┐
│      Old method (financial-driven)      │
├─────────────────────────────────────────┤
│         Return on Investment (ROI)      │
└─────────────────────────────────────────┘
                    ⬇
┌─────────────────────────────────────────┐
│      New method (comparison-driven)     │
├─────────────────────────────────────────┤
│        Return on Expectations (ROE)     │
└─────────────────────────────────────────┘
```

Based on extensive research, comparison of program success, and analysis of existing TE/TI/TROI measurement models, I conceptualized a simple, intuitive, and practical 4-tier model. The foundational premise of this model is that it is not about

CH 2 - MEASURING LARGE SCALE TECHNICAL TRAINING

what you are measuring. It is all about 'expectations' from a given training program. Hence, the key question is:

> ***Does this training program generate enough Return on Expectations?***

Therefore, instead of investment, we are measuring training corresponding to the impact it will create. That is why the model is named as **Return on Expectations (ROE)** Model. This model is geared toward the language of ratios and indices, which is already familiar to engineers and technical managers. The main use of this model is to measure TE in a systematic engineering way.

At first, the model looks like generic or popular models like Kirkpatrick's model. While philosophically, it has a similar number of levels, the methodology is far more common-sense and practical.

The idea of the ROE model is to provide a practical method of measuring TE based on 'common-sense' business metrics technical training and engineering program leaders use in the normal course of work without trying to develop their business or financial acumen.

3

AN INTUITIVE MODEL FOR TECHNICAL TRAINING MANAGERS

TRAINING IMPACT MEASUREMENT

A COMMON-SENSE MODEL FOR ENGINEERS

Based on my research, I came up with a simplified and practical TE/TI/TROI measurement framework, that is the 4-tier Return on Expectations (ROE) model for engineers. This model measures learning and on-the-job performance resulting from several support factors and provides impact measures in the form of four indexes. It has 4-tiers, in line with the most popular TE/TI/TROI measurement models, to keep a similar philosophical stand but propose a more practical common-sense methodology.

> **Tier 1: Reaction Index (RI)** - measures how well employees respond to a training program and their overall satisfaction with it.
>
> **Tier 2: Improvement Index (II)** - measures the relative improvement in employees' skills and knowledge after the training program.
>
> **Tier 3: Effectiveness Index (EI)** - measures the overall effectiveness of training program in achieving business goals.
>
> **Tier 4: Impact Index (ImI)** - measures the actual impact of training program on business performance and outcomes.

CH 3 - AN INTUITIVE MODEL

Practicality of indexes

Traditional TE/TI/TROI measurement models often rely on complex models and frameworks that can be difficult to understand and apply in practice. Indexes, on the other hand, provide a simple, numerical representation of the impact of training on employee performance and business outcomes. A comparison of three major models, Kirkpatrick's model, Philips' ROI model, and my ROE model, is given in Table 5.

Table 5: Comparison of three TE/TI/TROI measurement models

	Kirkpatrick evaluation model	Phillips' ROI model	Attri's ROE model
Based on	4 levels of results during and after training	The concept of 'return on investment'	The concept of 'return on expectations' instead of 'return on investment'
Level 1	Reaction	Reaction	Reaction Index
Level 2	Learning	Learning	Improvement Index
Level 3	Behavior	Behavior	Effectiveness Index
Level 4	Results (impact)	Results (impact)	Impact Index
Level 5	-	ROI	-

TRAINING IMPACT MEASUREMENT

As you see, rather than chasing the ROI in terms of investment and outcome with actual dollars, the 4-tier ROE model provides a simpler and more practical approach to TE/TI/TROI measurement.

This model provides a simpler, feedback-driven process based on the standard operating practices a business typically adopts instead of inventing some new processes. Indexes are also more practical because they can be easily computed using data that is readily available from employee performance data sources and business performance metrics. This makes it easier for organizations to implement a system for measuring TE and tracking progress over time.

Measuring TE/TI/TROI through indexes is more practical because it provides a clear and concise way to quantify the results of a training program. It also emphasizes the importance of measuring both employee performance and business outcomes to assess the impact of training programs accurately.

Further, since this model provides effective results in the form of quarterly indexes and improvement trends, it makes a quicker connection with the executives to realize the value of training programs. Thus, the ROE approach focuses on key indicators of training success and is easy to explain to upper management.

Additionally, indexes can be customized and tailored to specific business needs and objectives. For example, an organization

CH 3 - AN INTUITIVE MODEL

may choose to focus on specific performance indicators critical to its business model rather than trying to apply a generic framework to all training programs.

Overall, using indexes to measure TE/TI/TROI is more practical, efficient, and effective than relying on complex models that may not be tailored to the specific needs of the organization.

4-TIER REPRESENTATION OF ROE MODEL

Figure 11 shows a simplified representation, while Figure 12 outlines the details of each level in the form of a pyramid, which is a typical representation used for TE/TI/TROI measurement models.

As you would notice, the pyramid is constructed by keeping level 1 on the top. The reason for that is as you go toward level 4, the relevance and importance of impact increases from an organizational standpoint. Thus, the pyramid represents the relative value of training as one goes toward the base of the pyramid.

TRAINING IMPACT MEASUREMENT

Figure 11: Model of 4-tiers for measurement of TE

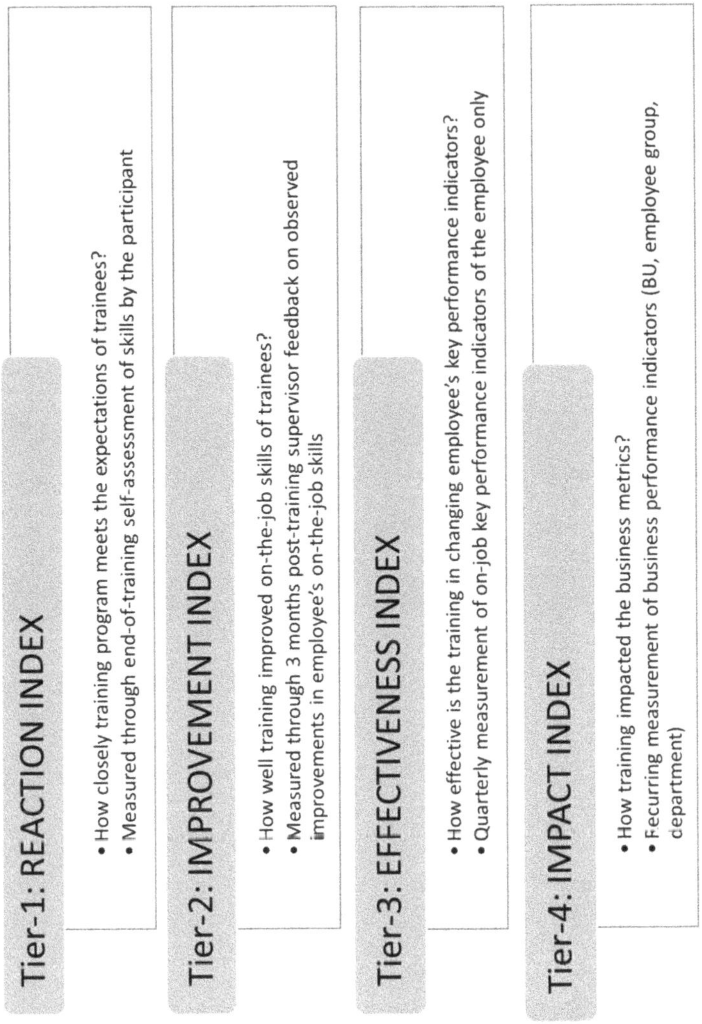

Tier-1: REACTION INDEX
- How closely training program meets the expectations of trainees?
- Measured through end-of-training self-assessment of skills by the participant

Tier-2: IMPROVEMENT INDEX
- How well training improved on-the-job skills of trainees?
- Measured through 3 months post-training supervisor feedback on observed improvements in employee's on-the-job skills

Tier-3: EFFECTIVENESS INDEX
- How effective is the training in changing employee's key performance indicators?
- Quarterly measurement of on-job key performance indicators of the employee only

Tier-4: IMPACT INDEX
- How training impacted the business metrics?
- Recurring measurement of business performance indicators (BU, employee group, department)

CH 3 – AN INTUITIVE MODEL

Figure 12: Detailed model of 4-tiers for measurement of TE

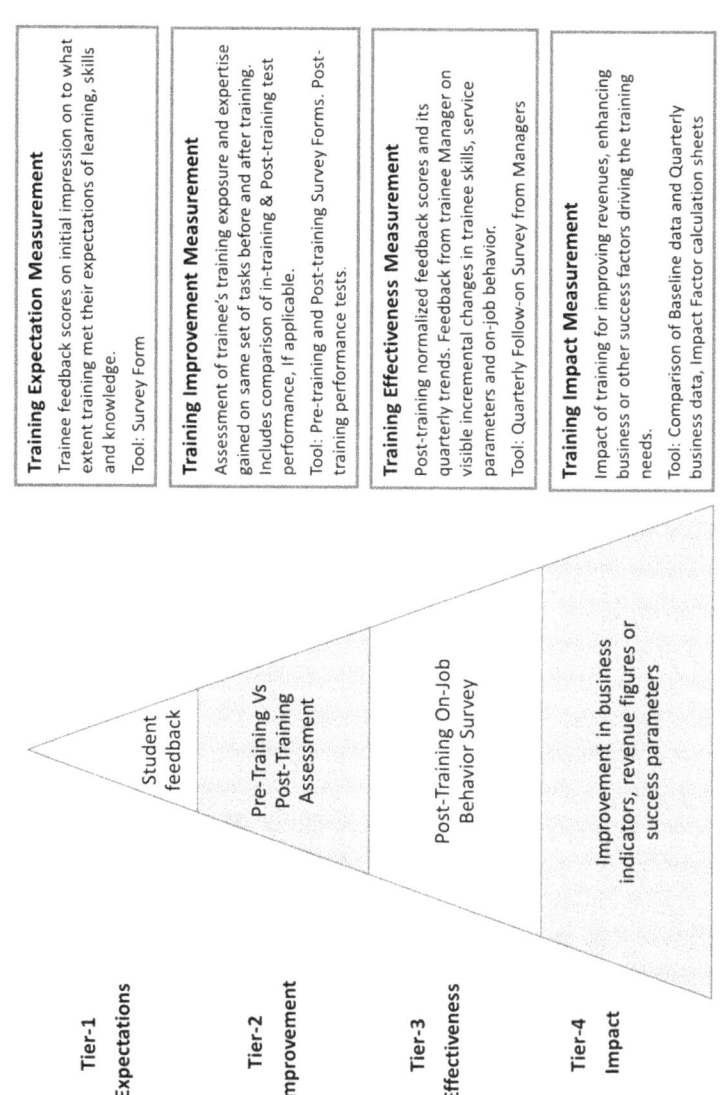

4

DATA COLLECTION IN ROE MODEL

TRAINING IMPACT MEASUREMENT

DATA COLLECTION

Even with a simplified framework, businesses may still face challenges in measuring TE/TI/TROI on a large scale. One of the main challenges is data collection and analysis, as this can be time-consuming and expensive, especially for businesses with a large workforce or multiple training programs. Additionally, it may be difficult to define and measure specific performance metrics for certain job roles or industries, making it challenging to accurately assess the impact of training programs.

To overcome these challenges, businesses may need to take a more strategic and systematic approach to measure TE/TI/TROI, including developing standardized processes and data collection methods. They may also need to invest in technology and tools that can automate and streamline data collection and analysis, making it easier and more cost-effective to measure the impact of training programs over time.

Leverage Day-to-Day data

The 4-tier ROE model involves a good amount of systematic data collection. However, what separates this model from any other is that it does not enforce training managers or business managers to work out different operating systems or gather a different set of data which they usually would do in the normal course of business. Rather, it looks for reasonable data generated during routine daily operations. The model takes data that business managers and executives typically use to review business status. Thus, you do not need to conduct any additional cumbersome analysis or isolation of factors to show your training program's value.

However, like any other data analytics exercise, it does require a disciplined implementation of a framework for data collection to objectivity. I established a 6-step systematic data collection in the ROE model, as shown in Table 6. These steps are not prescriptive but guidelines that can be applied flexibly depending upon the nature of the business.

The data collection flow and the corresponding computation of indices are shown in Figure 13.

Table 6: Six steps of data collection for measuring TE/TI/TROI

Step	Goal	What to Collect
1	COMPETENCY MAP FROM JOB PERFORMANCE METRICS	i. Job performance metrics ii. Skill/ knowledge competency maps
2	PRE-TRAINING BASELINE	i. Business performance ii. Employee performance iii. Employee pre-training self-assessment
3	POST-TRAINING SELF-ASSESSMENT	i. Employee confidence and competence against skills/competency map

TRAINING IMPACT MEASUREMENT

4	POST-TRAINING SUPERVISOR'S ASSESSMENT	i.	Quarterly assessment of an employee's skills/knowledge by the supervisor
		ii.	Performance data from company sources and operations
5	QUARTERLY JOB PERFORMANCE	i.	Averaged/normalized data of seasoned employees
		ii.	Averaged/normalized data of new employees
6	QUARTERLY BUSINESS PERFORMANCE INDICATORS	i.	Business performance of the business unit, metrics, and results, like profits, sales, revenues, escalations handled, cost savings, and so forth. Financial or non-financial data like customer satisfaction, customer retention, and time-to-resolution of a problem

These six steps are described in detail in the following sections. For an exact application and a real-world case study, refer to Chapter 9.

CH 4 - DATA COLLECTION IN ROE MODEL

Figure 13: Data collection flow and indices

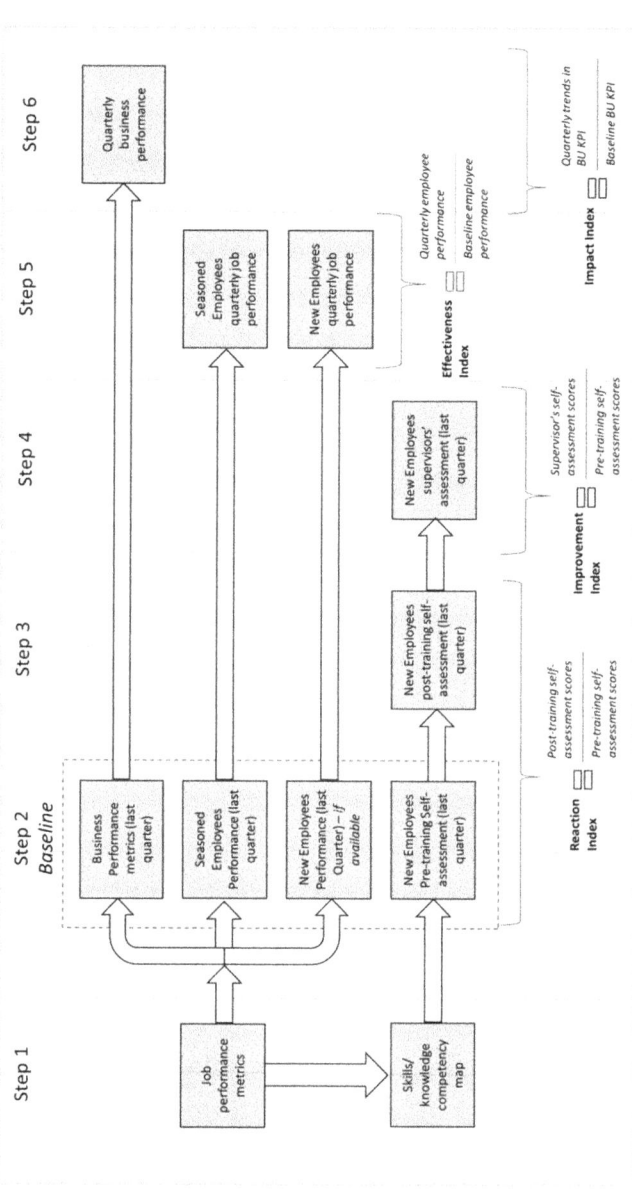

TRAINING IMPACT MEASUREMENT

STEP 1: COMPETENCY MAP FROM JOB PERFORMANCE METRICS

What to collect

At step 1, you need two critical pieces of data: 1) job performance metrics and 2) skills or knowledge required to attain those metrics.

> **1. Job performance metrics:**
>
> As the first step, develop the blueprints of targeted job role. List out all the performance metrics used to measure success in that role.
>
> **2. Skills/knowledge competency map:**
>
> Draw a list or map of skills and knowledge required to perform the identified job role.
>
> The traditional approach is to list out skills or knowledge to perform an identified job role in the form of a list or table. However, that process includes several skills irrelevant to the job performance. So, focus on building a visual map of how skills certainly contribute toward attaining the outcomes in a job role. In other words, how identified skills lead to the job performance metrics.

CH 4 – DATA COLLECTION IN ROE MODEL

Keep in mind that this is not traditional 'skill-need analysis,' rather it is an 'outcome-need analysis.' For instance, if the performance metric is to produce sales of $1 million a quarter, the traditional approach would list things like understanding product features, general sales process/negotiation skills, and using enterprise software or systems.

However, mastery of these things is not a sure-shot recipe for attaining $1 million in sales. Thus, for measurement purposes, we must focus only on those skills and knowledge (or competencies) that indeed lead to a $1 million sales goal.

Therefore, the actual list may include using an institution's infrastructure to locate repeat customers, organizational-specific networking avenues, using established tools, and similar skills proven to give results. The focus of such competency maps must be on the outcomes, not on the skills. Such a goal can be achieved when we start with outcomes and build a map of necessary skills to attain our goal.

When to collect

This should be a one-time exercise for each job role. But this is unlike those stationary job descriptions which are rarely changed for decades in organizations. Instead, there can be an annual HR exercise to make sure skill maps stay relevant to the new performance metrics or evolving needs in the organization.

Who will collect

Normally, it would be the direct manager who will conduct job analysis. However, in my experience, most HR professionals and direct managers are rarely qualified to do the skill map we need for measurement purposes.

There is usually a disconnection between how job competencies are viewed by HR professionals vs. direct managers. For example, job analysis of a sales job for an HR professional may mean breaking it down into roles, responsibilities, tasks, skills, knowledge, and experience. But from a direct manager's point of view, such a breakdown would mean listing the ability of employees to navigate the dynamics of the job, integrate different skills/knowledge together, use internal and external resources, conduct not only financial analysis but also emotional analysis of the customers to make a successful sale.

Later are the kind of skills/knowledge that need to be identified to make a competency map. In reality, this should be a joint exercise between HR and departmental heads of functional units.

CH 4 – DATA COLLECTION IN ROE MODEL

Where used

This competency map should be the basis for developing training programs for employees. A training program not aligned to the skill/knowledge map and not leading to attaining the required job metrics or outcome will not meet the business goals.

This competency map is also used to design a pre-training rating survey that asks incoming employees before training to assess their confidence and competence in skills/knowledge on the survey.

STEP 2: PRE-TRAINING BASELINE

What to collect

At this step, you need two types of data. 1) the business performance baseline of the business unit, 2) the baseline performance of employees in all the job roles within that business unit, and 3) the employees pre-training self-assessment baseline.

> 1. *Business performance:*
>
>   Collect and baseline data on key business performance indicators of the target business unit.

TRAINING IMPACT MEASUREMENT

It should include those indicators which determine the performance of that business unit.

2. *Employee performance:*

Gather data on performance indicators of the employees within the identified business unit. This data include the performance metrics against which an employee's job is measured or tracked. It conveys how employees are performing against those metrics before taking a training program.

There are a few types of data that can be collected:

a. <u>Seasoned Employees Baseline Performance:</u> The first category of data you will need is the employee performance data measured and averaged across all the seasoned employees performing a job role. This becomes the baseline threshold that the new employees are 'expected' to demonstrate in due course of time after training.

How near are the new employees to this threshold after a training program is an indication of the effectiveness or impact of that program.

Care should be taken to define the time period for a cutline. It depends upon the time taken by seasoned employees to attain the required proficiency. Ideally, one year of employee performance is a good baseline to set the targets for new employees.

b. <u>New Employees Baseline Performance</u>: The second type of data you will need is the performance data measured and averaged across new employees performing a job role.

However, in most instances, such data may not be available. Certain jobs require employees to get fully trained and certified before they can perform the job or be considered ready to produce the outcomes. In such cases, it is not advisable to collect this data.

In some cases, employees may already be hired with appropriate skills for the job, while training courses are meant to provide them with task-specific or organization-specific skills. In such cases, performance data of new employees can be gathered at the individual employee level. But it is not required for the baseline.

TRAINING IMPACT MEASUREMENT

3. Employee pre-training self-assessment:

Each employee slated to go for a specific training program needs to complete a self-assessment on their current skills/knowledge targeted in that training program. This allows for assessing their current confidence and competence in skills required to do the job. Keep in mind that confidence conveys one's assumption of being able to do a task, while competence is the demonstration of being able to do the said task. Thus, both confidence and competence must be assessed for a complete picture of their current standing.

This data is averaged across all new employees serving that specific job role and aggregated over a quarter forming the baseline self-assessment.

Data at the individual employee level will also be useful to the direct manager for development purposes but may not be required from a TE measurement standpoint.

When to collect

Timing for the baseline is very important to make sure you take proper reference of comparison. Often, an organization baseline a specific quarter and then continue to compare data for subsequent quarters against that baseline. With that approach, you may run into the reference of comparison, which is no longer contextual.

Employee Performance data baseline timing

For instance, if you have baselined the employee performance in Q1, you might be using it to compare the post-training performance during Q4. Doing so means you are ignoring or downplaying the effect of several initiatives that may already have improved employee performance during Q2 and Q3. Thus, you are showing a massive improvement in employee performance post-training in Q4. Therefore, it is recommended that your baseline should be revised continuously to the last completed quarter. That will consider the recency effect.

Timing of business performance data baseline

For business performance, it is again advisable to refer to the last quarter's data as the baseline instead of baselining once.

Timing of employee self-assessment data baseline

For the self-assessment baseline, ideally, this data should be collected immediately before the start of a training program. You can couple such collection through automated tools to trigger

TRAINING IMPACT MEASUREMENT

surveys just prior to the assigned training events. Note that such an arrangement will collect employees' individual data, which still needs to be averaged over all employees going to the training.

If a training program is offered continuously, or scheduled at regular intervals to cater to various groups of new employees, then the best is to take the previous quarter's collective data for all the employees who undertook training.

Who will collect

o   Employees (source)
o   Managers (source)
o   Business units (coordinate all)

Where used

This data is used as a baseline reference to compare with post-training data measured against the same set of metrics. The comparison leads to computing the 'Reaction Index' in Tier-1 of the ROE model. Details of the Reaction Index are covered in Chapter 5.

CH 4 – DATA COLLECTION IN ROE MODEL

STEP 3: POST-TRAINING SELF-ASSESSMENT

What to collect

Employees who just finished training are asked to complete the same self-assessment used at the pre-training stage. They are asked to rate their confidence and competence against the same skills/competency map.

The data is then averaged/normalized across the entire group of new employees if it is a one-time training event.

If training is offered on a regular basis for an influx of employees, then this data should be averaged across all new employees who received training in that quarter.

This data may have additional use by breaking it down to each employee level to analyze specific development gaps.

When to collect

Post-training self-assessment should be administered at the end of the training program if it contains multiple training events. Sometimes, it is advisable to give the trainees a week's gestation period to reflect upon what they learned, so the self-assessment is more conservative than an instant overshooting of confidence during the training.

TRAINING IMPACT MEASUREMENT

Who will collect

- Training instructors
- Training managers
- Direct managers

Where used

Data collected at this step is then compared with the same set of baseline reference data collected in Step 2. The comparison leads to computing the 'Reaction Index' in Tier-1 of the ROE model.

STEP 4: POST-TRAINING SUPERVISOR'S ASSESSMENT

What to collect

At this step, the primary data needed is the supervisor's quarterly assessment of an employee's skills/knowledge.

For this data, the same assessment tool is used, which was used by employees for self-assessment during the pre-training stage (Step 2) and post-training stage (Step 3).

However, at this step, the supervisor is required to fill it up based on rationale evidence from several performance data sources. The idea is that the performance metrics should be used as objective measures to ascertain an employee's skills/knowledge rating. This is not a subjective rating by a supervisor, so this stage does not involve assigning performance ratings to employees. Generally, the performance rating data has no direct relevance to training impact measurement.

The data from all the supervisors whose employees have received training within that quarter is averaged across all the employees throughout the past quarter.

Who will collect

o   Direct managers

When to collect

This exercise is repeated on a rolling basis at the end of each quarter. Though new employees are rated each quarter, the quarter-over-quarter data represents how well the workforce is improving overall.

Where to collect from

The rationale and evidence-based sources a manager can use depend upon business operations and systems used by the organization. A manager could use data sources such as customer relationship management systems, escalation matrices, customer complaints, task trackers, customer

TRAINING IMPACT MEASUREMENT

satisfaction scores, stakeholder 360-degree feedback, project success sheets, balanced scorecards, etc.

Where used

This data is used to compute the Improvement Index (II) of the ROE model. It indicates relative improvement in an employee's skills/knowledge based on evidence from various organizational data sources.

STEP 5: QUARTERLY JOB PERFORMANCE

What to collect

In this step, you will collect data separately for all seasoned and new employees who have recently received training. That way, you have two reference points for comparison. This data is averaged/normalized across two segments of employees – seasoned and new.

Where to collect from

Data is collected against the job performance metrics used in Step 1 to draw a skills/knowledge competency map. For example, for a call center job, call duration, number of calls handled per hour, quality scores, and time-to-resolution metrics may be gathered to determine success in that job role.

CH 4 – DATA COLLECTION IN ROE MODEL

A manager can use data sources such as customer relationship management systems, escalation matrices, customer complaints, task trackers, customer satisfaction scores, stakeholder 360-degree feedback, project success sheets, balanced scorecards etc.

Given that employee job performance is typically measured with multiple key performance indicators (KPIs), you need to map it or transform it into one number to make inferences and comparisons.

One typical approach to working out a single number is to use a balanced scorecard (BSC). Depending upon the nature of the business or how you measure organizational performance, you may have to institute a balanced scorecard process on employee quarterly performance.

But as we see, most organizations do not use balance score card on employee performance measurements. An easy workaround would be to apply a balanced scorecard only on employee performance, even if executives do not mandate it.

Another approach could be assigning weights to each KPI and computing a single number using a weighted average.

Who will collect

- Direct managers
- Business unit owner

TRAINING IMPACT MEASUREMENT

When to collect

Collect each quarter on a rolling basis if a continuous influx of employees receives training. Make this data collection part of the standard operations review and standard operating procedure. Managers can keep gathering this every quarter by segmenting the employees into seasoned and new buckets.

Where used

This data is used to compare with the baseline data for employee performance to compute the Effectiveness Index in Tier-3 of the ROE model.

New employees' quarterly performance data is compared to their pre-training baseline data to see how their Effectiveness Index has improved within that segment.

At the same time, new employees' quarterly performance data is compared with the seasoned employees' quarterly performance data to complete the picture regarding how closely a training program is meeting the objectives of transforming the abilities of new employees into abilities possessed by seasoned employees.

STEP 6: QUARTERLY BUSINESS PERFORMANCE INDICATORS

What to collect

At this stage, the business performance of the business unit is gathered, which may include the metrics and results that a business unit is responsible for delivering. Examples are profits, sales, revenues, escalations handled, cost savings, and so forth.

Business performance may not always be financial or monetary, depending upon the nature of the department's business. For example, for a call center's tech support group, the business results will be an improvement in customer satisfaction, customer retention, and time-to-resolution of a problem.

When to collect

Quarterly or whatever the business reporting cycle is used in an organization should already be standard practice in most business organizations.

Who will collect

o   Business unit owners

TRAINING IMPACT MEASUREMENT

Where used

This data is used with three indices computed in Tier-1 to Tier-3 of the ROE model. Quarterly trends are plotted among indices, employee performance metrics, and business unit performance data. These trends provide a highly enriched picture of the collective impact of training programs.

The most critical KPIs are identified, and then the ratio of value is computed with reference to the baseline established in Step 1. This step calculates the Impact Index. Depending on the business, Impact Index may not always be computable.

5
MEASURING REACTION INDEX

TRAINING IMPACT MEASUREMENT

Reaction Index: How closely does a training program meet the expectations of trainees?

WHY REACTION INDEX

Traditional models of measuring student reaction in training programs often focus on subjective feedback, such as how the participants felt about training. However, this approach may not provide a clear picture of how well the training program meets the expectations of trainees in terms of on-the-job performance.

To address this issue, the first tier of the ROE model, called the 'Reaction Index (RI)', measures the improvement in the perceived skills and knowledge of the participants. This measurement is based on self-assessment ratings collected from each trainee at the end of the training class using a well-drafted instrument. The scores are based on the trainees' perceived confidence and competence level in the specified on-the-job skills.

To use this information effectively, a pre-training baseline self-assessment survey is conducted on the same skills before trainees attend a training program. The baseline scores and the post-training self-assessment scores are then used to compute the Reaction Index, which is the ratio of the average self-

CH 5 – MEASURING REACTION INDEX

assessment scores after the training program to the average scores taken before the training.

THE PROCESS

- Objective: Measure improvement in perceived skills/knowledge
- Who: Training Participants
- When: At the end of training
- Outcome: Reaction Index
- Source: Pre-training baseline scores and post-training self-assessment
- Data collection: Step 2 and Step 3

Measurement

This tier measures the training reaction with self-assessment rating scores collected from each trainee at the end of training class using a well-drafted instrument. Several of the popular TE/TE/TROI measurement models advocate the same thing. So, what is new in this model?

Traditional models emphasize measuring trainees' reaction and how they 'feel' about training. In complex business settings, your goal as a technical training manager is to get how soon your trainees become ready for the job. You are interested in the results which impact the business. You would not want to take a smiley sheet 'how well a trainer taught the class

TRAINING IMPACT MEASUREMENT

objectives' and things like that. You would be interested to know the progress trainees have made toward on-the-job performance.

Data collection

Employees come to a training event to learn those on-the-job skills that can make them successful in a shorter time. That is what their 'expectations' are. What you want to do is to measure how well you meet those expectations. However, we are not talking about subjective expectations and what they want from a training event.

With changing business needs, measuring the confidence and competence gained by trainees from a training event on the specified on-the-job skills makes sense. At this stage, you can ask learners to self-assess the knowledge and skills they just acquired in the training program. This is Step 2 of data collection. This measurement measures their 'perceived' confidence and competence level. These scores can be normalized or calibrated by the instructor's measurement of their skills as indicated by formative or non-formative training assessments. This quantitatively measures their readiness for on-the-job assignments for which they came to attend the training program.

The data collection flow to compute the Reaction Index is shown in Figure 14.

CH 5 - MEASURING REACTION INDEX

Figure 14: Data collection and flow for Reaction Index

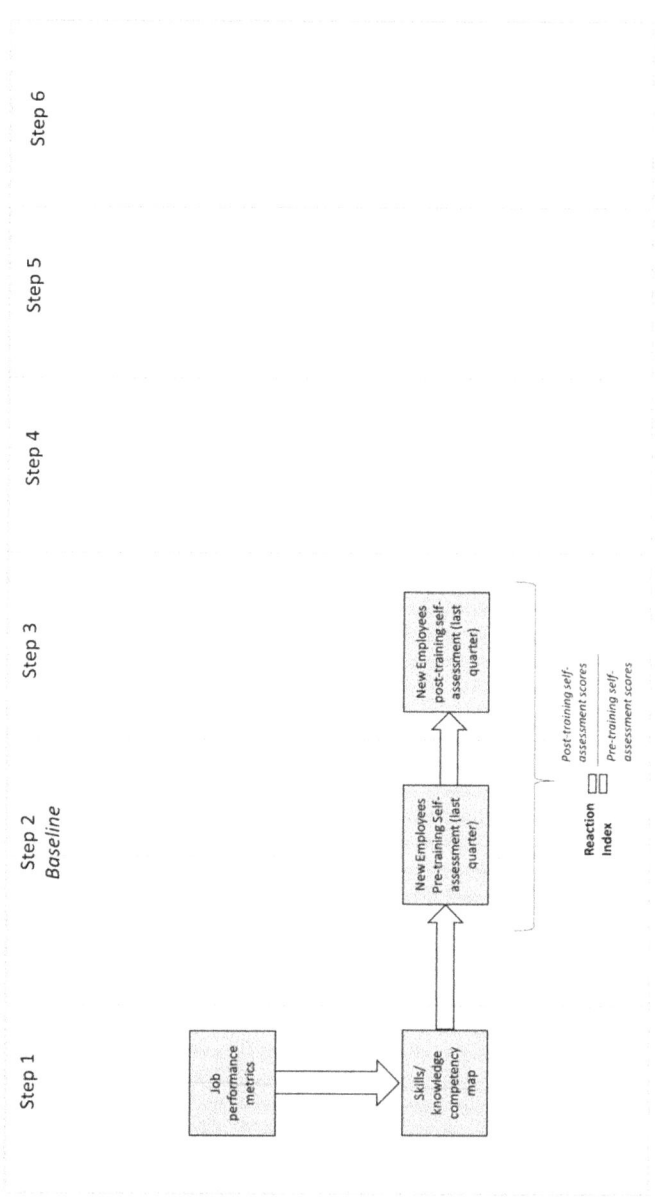

TRAINING IMPACT MEASUREMENT

Applying the Model

In simple words, the higher the scores of this self-assessment are, the closer you are to providing them with the skills required to do the job and eventually meet the business needs.

To use this information to improve your training alignment with business, you first need to conduct a self-assessment survey (pre-training baseline self-assessment) on the same skills/measures before trainees come to the training program. This is indicated as Step 1 of data collection. That data will give you the baseline scores of their pre-training skills/knowledge.

With the pre-training baseline self-assessment scores and the post-training self-assessment of confidence and competence, you can compute an index called the 'Reaction Index.' This Index is the ratio of the average self-assessment scores of an employee in pre-defined skills/knowledge after the training program to the average self-assessment scores for the same set of skills/knowledge taken before the training.

$$\text{REACTION INDEX} = \frac{\text{Post-training self-assessment scores}}{\text{Pre-training baseline self-assessment score}}$$

Inferences from Reaction Index

While Reaction Index is based on the perception of participants and may not reflect reality, it is still an important measure that

CH 5 - MEASURING REACTION INDEX

can be validated through subsequent tiers of the ROE model. Ideally, Reaction Index should be > 1.

As shown in Table 7, a large Reaction Index means that the training program has high relevance to the participants, and their training aligns well with the way they see their on-the-job challenges.

However, if the Reaction Index is less than 1, it may indicate that the scope of training needs to be reassessed, and the measurement instrument should be reviewed to ensure that it reflects on-the-job requirements correctly.

Table 7: Interpreting Reaction Index

Improvement Index	Interpretation	Action
More than 1	The training program is aligned well with the way they see their on-the-job challenges.	-
Less than 1	The training program may not be representative of the on-the-job challenges.	The scope of training needs to be reassessed.

Check out Chapter 9 for a real-world case study application.

6
MEASURING IMPROVEMENT INDEX

TRAINING IMPACT MEASUREMENT

Improvement Index: How well has training improved the on-the-job skills of trainees?

WHY IMPROVEMENT INDEX

The traditional way of measuring student performance improvement in a training program has been to rely on subjective ratings or 'feel-based' assessments. This approach does not accurately measure the skills and knowledge gained by the trainee, nor does it offer a clear understanding of how these skills translate into on-the-job performance.

To address this issue, the ROE model offers a new way of measuring student improvement called the 'Improvement Index.' This second tier of the model focuses on measuring observed improvement in on-the-job skills because of a training program. Improvement Index is an objective measure of improvement collected from a supervisor's assessment of the employee's job performance three months after the training program.

CH 6 – MEASURING IMPROVEMENT INDEX

THE PROCESS

- Objective: Measure observed improvement in on-the-job skills because of a training program
- Who: Employee's supervisor
- When: 3 months after training
- Outcome: Improvement Index (II)
- Source: Employee performance data sources
- Data collection: Step 4

To compute the Improvement Index, data is collected from various sources, including a company's customer relationship management database, escalation matrix, task trackers, customer satisfaction scores, stakeholder 360-degree feedback, project success sheets, balanced scorecards etc. These data inputs are consolidated to form a composite picture of the employee's confidence and competence in the skills and knowledge displayed in the field.

Measurement

When an employee does his job and applies the skills or behavior they learned during training, a supervisor is bound to notice some visible indicators of changes in his job behavior, skills, and attitudes. Though there are several factors, including the influence of the direct manager, success during the first three months can be safely attributed to skills learned in the

TRAINING IMPACT MEASUREMENT

training program. But the first three months are short enough to establish the course's long-term effectiveness or its impact on the business. Therefore, you need an intermediate measure called 'improvement' with a measurement instrument (survey based on job performance data) to be put in place within three months of training program.

Data collection

The complex organizational settings make use of a single instrument infeasible. Therefore, you may have to use an integrated system that combines data inputs (qualitative and quantitative) from various sources, as mentioned before, like a company's customer relationship management database, escalation matrix, task trackers, customer satisfaction scores, stakeholder 360-degree feedback, project success sheets, balanced scorecards, etc.

Data from these sources can be consolidated to form a composite picture for a supervisor to objectively or rationally rate the confidence and competence of the employee in the skills/knowledge displayed by him three months after the training.

However, such methods fail when a supervisor is asked to provide a subjective 'feel-based' rating without the context of business metrics from different sources or when just one source of data is used to work out the ratings.

CH 6 - MEASURING IMPROVEMENT INDEX

The data collection flow to compute Improvement Index is shown in Figure 15.

TRAINING IMPACT MEASUREMENT

Figure 15: Data collection and flow for Improvement Index

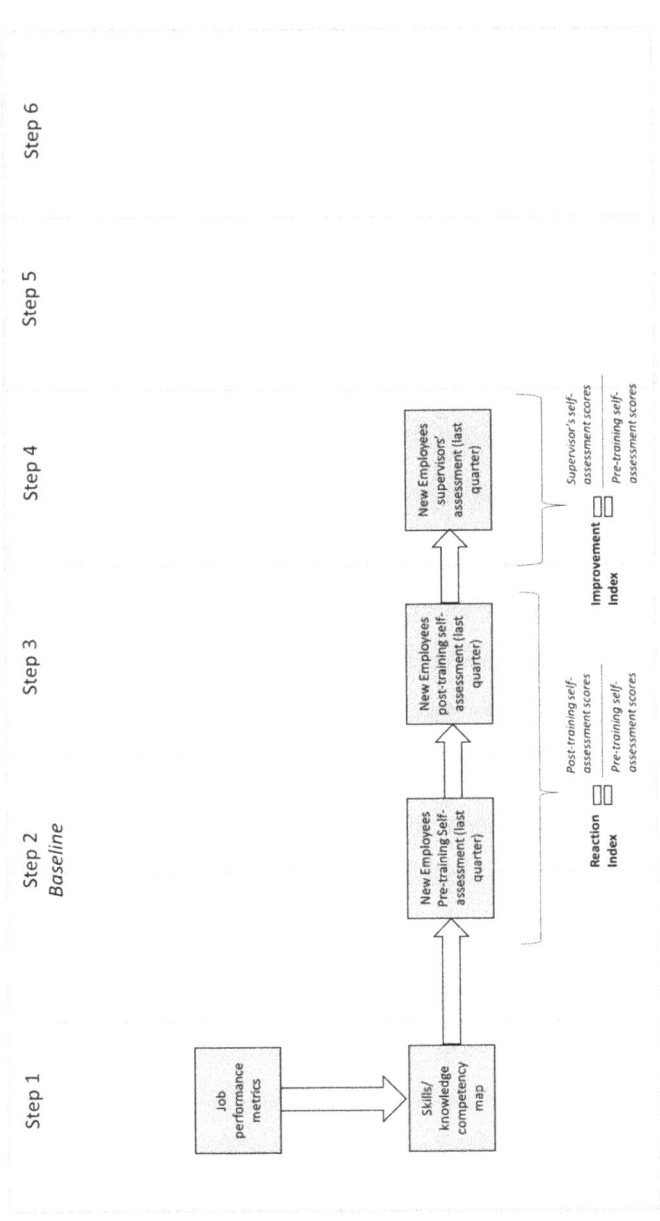

CH 6 – MEASURING IMPROVEMENT INDEX

Applying the model

You can use this information to compute the Improvement Index for a training program.

$$\text{IMPROVEMENT INDEX} = \frac{\text{3-month supervisor's assessment scores}}{\text{Pre-training baseline self-assessment score}}$$

This instrument is primarily for the supervisors and should be aligned very well with the pre-training baseline self-assessment (in Step 1 of data collection) and with the post-training self-assessment (in Step 2 of data collection). Here we have isolated the measurements from any 'business results' measurement at this point. The premise is first to establish the fact that training indeed resulted in an improvement of skills for the trained employees before we measure training's impact on the business.

This exercise generates the measure of the observed performance of the employee in terms of skills (not in terms of business indicators) in the field. This data would show you the improvement attained after training and how it is improving over time. This exercise will give a 'relative' improvement before and after training in terms of meaningful acquired and applied skills, improvement in attitudes, enhancement of knowledge, level of handling of assignments, and level of fulfillment of the supervisor's expectations.

TRAINING IMPACT MEASUREMENT

Inferences from Reaction Index and Improvement Index

You can compare this value to the Reaction Index computed using the same set of skills. By rule, the training Improvement Index should be more than Reaction Index due to field exposure and an increase in confidence.

As shown in Table 8, an ideal Improvement Index would be >1, indicating that the training program has significantly improved employees' skills and knowledge.

If the Improvement Index is 1, it means that training has shown no improvement in the skills yet, which could be a cause of concern, and you need to be careful.

If Reaction Index is lower than the Improvement Index, it could indicate that training is no longer effective. Post-training performance support systems and other supporting mechanisms do not reinforce the learning in training program. You have organizational trouble for which training is no longer a solution. Some other support mechanisms need to be put in place to reinforce the learning. This also tells another story: training may not have been correctly designed in line with field requirements or may have changed since the training.

By combining the Reaction Index and Improvement Index, the ROE model provides an assessment of the training program's effectiveness and whether it needs to be revisited.

CH 6 – MEASURING IMPROVEMENT INDEX

Table 8: Interpreting Improvement Index

Improvement Index	Interpretation	Action
More than 1	Training has created a meaningful improvement in the employee's skills and knowledge	-
Less than 1	Training has not created any positive improvement in the skills yet	Redesign training or continue gathering data
Reaction Index < Improvement Index	Organizational post-training support issues, training is no longer a solution	Rethink post-training support mechanisms

This approach offers a more accurate measure of student/employee performance improvement, providing technical training managers with valuable insights into the skills and knowledge acquired by trainees and how these skills translate into on-the-job performance.

Check out Chapter 9 for a real-world case study application.

7
MEASURING EFFECTIVENESS INDEX

TRAINING IMPACT MEASUREMENT

Effectiveness Index: How effective is training in changing employee performance parameters?

WHY EFFECTIVENESS INDEX

Traditional ways of measuring the effectiveness of training programs rely on assessing learners' reactions and feedback about the training they received. However, this approach fails to capture whether learners' skills and knowledge have actually improved and translated into improved job performance.

A new way is to focus on the true effectiveness of training. The third tier of the ROE model is particularly important as it goes beyond learners' reactions and feedback. Instead, the 'Effectiveness Index (EI)' measures the impact of training on key performance indicators such as service time, call duration, productivity, and customer satisfaction scores. Using pre-training employee performance baseline and quarterly performance data, Effectiveness Index provides a quantified assessment of training's impact on employees' job performance.

CH 7 – MEASURING EFFECTIVENESS INDEX

THE PROCESS

- Objective: Measure the impact of training on employee performance indicators
- Who: Employee's supervisor
- When: Quarterly
- Outcome: Effectiveness Index
- Source: Employee performance data sources
- Data collection step: Step 5

Measurement

By now, you already have a good idea of improvement in skills introduced by training in the employee group. If Improvement Index is over 1, you need to move forward to see if employees have produced meaningful and measurable business or job-specific results using their skills learned during the training program (or improvised in the field). This is a collective assessment made by the supervisor and business unit (BU) owners regarding the quantifiable impact on employee performance indicators due to training.

Data collection

Instead of a numeric scale, a data-driven approach is adopted at this stage. Data can be collected from the organization or BU's CRM/ SAP or other integrated database repositories, which track performance data for each business transaction by

TRAINING IMPACT MEASUREMENT

employees. Some examples of parameters indicating an employee's performance are service time, call duration, time to repair, time-to-resolution, productivity per unit of time, the number of closures, case closure times, customer satisfaction scores, success rates etc. This data should be gathered as a baseline during the pre-training exercise (Step 1) and later on a quarterly basis (Step 5).

Employee performance parameters used here should be the ones that were used to draw the list of skills/knowledge targeted in a program, used in pre-training baseline measurements and post-training expectation measurements. The tough part is mapping the skills to on-the-job performance indicators. However, if a good job has been done to ensure that training objectives reflect the real-world performance of the employee group, then the mapping would be easy to do.

The data collection flow to compute the Effectiveness Index is shown in Figure 16.

CH 7 - MEASURING EFFECTIVENESS INDEX

Figure 16: Data collection and flow for Effectiveness Index

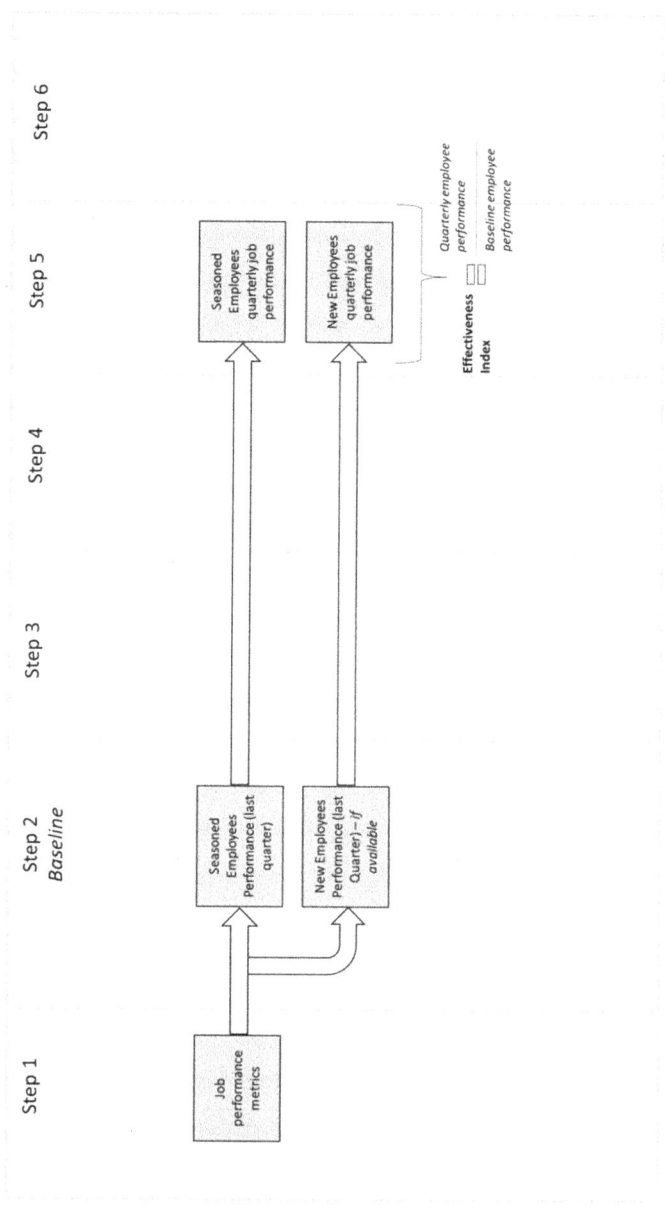

TRAINING IMPACT MEASUREMENT

Applying the model

This tier aims to gather the nearly 'quantified' impact of training on key performance indicators like time to service, person-hours, service cost, etc. Note that at this point, we are still not getting into the business unit's business performance collectively. If you want to measure the effectiveness, you need to first see the training's impact on employee performance indicators and not on the business unit's performance. In short, it is called the effectiveness of training in terms of making employees more productive for given business needs.

The above information can be used to compute the Effectiveness Index if the pre-training employee performance baseline data is available. This index measures how much training contributed to or affected meeting the individual employee's performance goals as a business contributor.

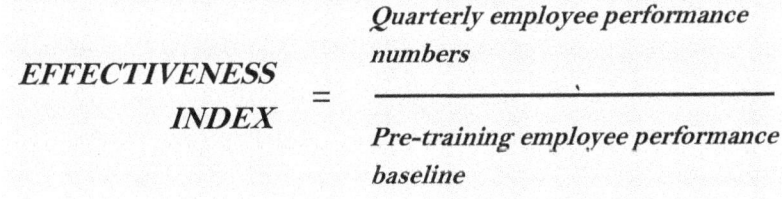

$$\text{EFFECTIVENESS INDEX} = \frac{\text{Quarterly employee performance numbers}}{\text{Pre-training employee performance baseline}}$$

What if an employee is new and baseline data does not exist? Well, in that case, the organization's average baseline data can be used. In some instances, using organizational baseline data on average is advisable to take an integrated business approach.

CH 7 - MEASURING EFFECTIVENESS INDEX

One key point to note here is that employee performance, if measured through multiple KPIs, needs to be first translated into one specific number. Usually, that number is found using a balanced scorecard. The purpose of the balanced scorecard is to assign a score based on achievements under multiple KPIs.

If your organization does not use a balanced scorecard process for employee performance, then you can compute the Effectiveness Index for each KPI of employee performance individually. If you chose the latter approach, be aware that now you will have multiple Effectiveness Indices, one for each KPI. Just need to make sure each KPI Index is greater than one. See the explanation below for the ideal value. Alternatively, you can combine multiple KPIs into one aggregated number by assigning weights to each KPI and summing it.

Inferences from three Indexes

An ideal Effectiveness Index is greater than 1, indicating that the training program effectively translates learners' improvements into measurable improvements in job performance. It also indicates that the training program is effective and designed correctly.

As suggested in Table 9, if Effectiveness Index is less than 1, that means that the training program is not effective in translating what they learned in training into job performance. You may need to re-assess the design of your training program.

TRAINING IMPACT MEASUREMENT

Table 9: Interpreting Effectiveness Index

Effectiveness Index	Interpretation	Action
More than 1	Training programs translate learners' improvements into improvements in job performance	-
Less than 1	Training program is not effective in translating into job performance	Re-assess the training design
High Improvement Index, Low Effectiveness Index	Training objectives are not aligned with on-the-job performance indicators	Re-assess if training objectives are truly drawn from on-the-job performance indicators
Low Improvement Index, High Effectiveness	Training is likely not a direct contributor toward improving employee performance indicators	Re-assess if employees truly need this training or if you could be better off without it

If the Improvement Index is high, but the Effectiveness Index is low, it suggests that the training objectives are not aligned with on-the-job performance indicators. You need to analyze whether training program objectives align with or are drawn from on-the-job performance indicators.

CH 7 - MEASURING EFFECTIVENESS INDEX

What if Improvement Index is low, but the Effectiveness Index is high? If you followed the actions to correct the low Improve Index, such a situation is improbable to arise.

But again, you can probably fix it for the subsequent traffic in training program. If the situation indeed happens for previously trained folks, then training is likely not a direct contributor toward improving the employee performance indicators.

Check out Chapter 9 for a real-world case study application.

8
MEASURING IMPACT INDEX

TRAINING IMPACT MEASUREMENT

Impact Index: To what extent has training impacted the business metrics specific to an employee group, business unit, or organization?

WHY IMPACT INDEX

Traditional methods of measuring training impact often focus on the training program itself without considering how it translates to real-world performance on the job. This can lead to a disconnect between training goals and business objectives. The fourth tier of the ROE model addresses this issue by measuring the impact of training on specific business metrics relevant to an employee group or business unit.

This is done by tracking the performance data of the business unit and comparing it to the pre-training baseline data. At this tier, it is not necessary to compute an index. However, for some instances, an 'Impact Index' may be feasible. Otherwise, the goal of this tier is on the quarterly trends in business performance.

CH 8 - MEASURING IMPACT INDEX

THE PROCESS

- o Objective: Measure the impact of training on employee group or BU or organization business KPIs
- o Who: BU owner
- o When: Quarterly (or based on business result reporting cycles)
- o Outcome: Impact Trends
- o Source: Business unit and organizational performance data sources
- o Data collection: Step 6

Measurement

If the measurement system implements the process discussed in the previous three tiers, then the business unit will have enough data which can be averaged and normalized quarterly over the entire organization for various training programs and business units. Now the three indices computed (averaged or normalized), i.e., Reaction Index, Improvement Index, and Effectiveness Index, can be plotted quarterly in relationship to the key performance indicators of a given business.

TRAINING IMPACT MEASUREMENT

Data collection

Every organization has some sort of metrics in place for tracking its performance. Some examples of business KPIs are start-to-close service time per call, cost per call, person-hours per case, the number of cases handled per employee, success rates of cases, and cost of labor per call etc.

The data collection flow to compute the Impact Index is shown in Figure 17.

Applying the model

During the training analysis exercise, training objectives are drawn from and mapped to the business indicators. Not all business indicators are used to develop the training program, and hence not all parameters are required to compute the impact of that training program. For example, for a repair-related business, the measurements should be related to the number of cases handled, revenue from the service, average hours spent in service, contract margins and so forth, as opposed to the organizational profit and loss.

If training program was aligned well with the business unit's objectives, then it makes sense to use the performance data of the business unit instead of the organization's performance data.

CH 8 - MEASURING IMPACT INDEX

Depending on the business unit's business model, it is possible to compute the Impact Index in relationship to some critical measurements.

$$IMPACT\ INDEX = \frac{\text{Post-training quarterly average of the selected KPI}}{\text{Baseline average of the selected KPI in a quarter prior to training}}$$

For example, if service call duration (SCD) is a critical business-driving factor, then we can plot the ratio of quarterly average of SCD regarding BU's baseline data on SCD measured at the pre-training stage.

Alternatively, we can plot the quarterly average SCD vs. the quarterly Effectiveness Index.

Briefly, the possibilities are endless, depending on the nature of the business. The measurement cycle should line up with the measurement cycle for business. If a business is monitored quarterly, then plotting this relationship quarterly makes sense.

Check out Chapter 9 for a real-world case study application.

TRAINING IMPACT MEASUREMENT

Figure 17: Data collection and flow for Impact Index

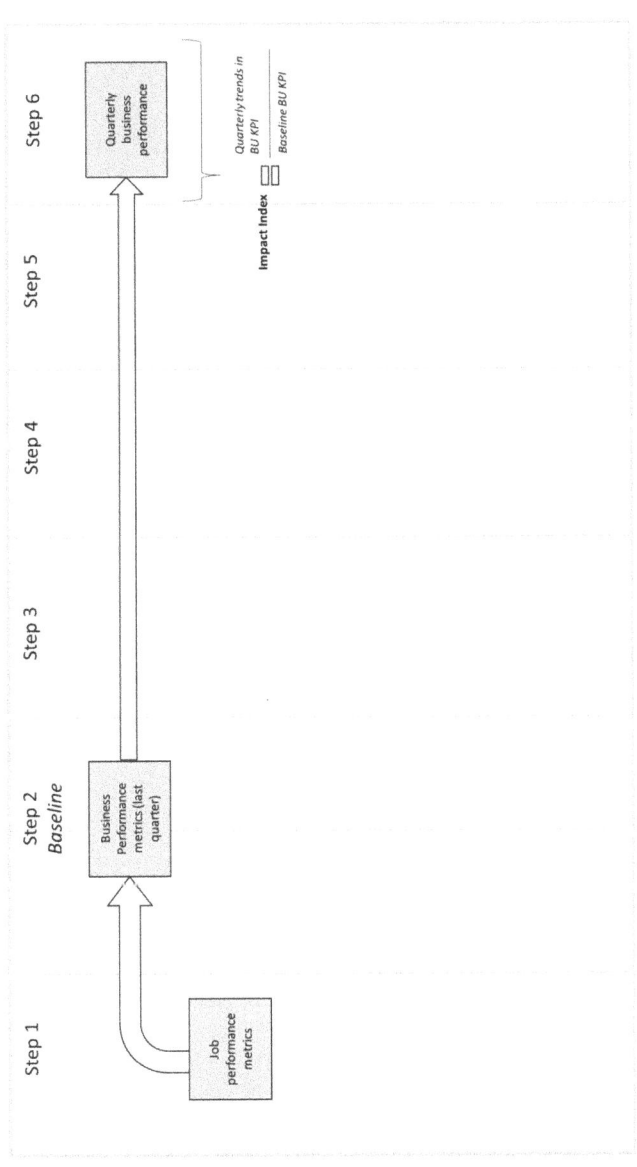

9
APPLYING THE MODEL IN PRACTICE

TRAINING IMPACT MEASUREMENT

THE BUSINESS

The company

A leading photocopier manufacturer is engaged in worldwide distribution and service of photocopier machines. As a manufacturer, their portfolio includes sales of photocopier machines and after-sales service support.

Business

The sales department handles the after-sales service through a dedicated service support department. Their service group employed over 500 employees worldwide who were qualified technicians.

For every machine they sell, they offer a separate post-warranty service contract that customers can renew annually. The contract price is negotiated based on the customer's needs. The contract outlines the binding on the service department to dispatch their service technicians within 24 hours of a machine issue reported by the customer.

A service contract assures customers that any machine problem would be resolved within 72 hours once an engineer is onsite. Customers can purchase premium contracts for after-office hours repair coverage, weekend coverage, and accelerated resolution of problems within 24 hours.

CH 9 - APPLYING THE MODEL IN PRACTICE

Hiring

Accordingly, photocopier technicians are hired to serve that obligation. Thus, they need to be fully qualified for the job. The repair department employs engineers based on business needs, the number of machines sold, and the capacity to serve the contracts. The more contracts sold, the more engineers are hired.

Training schedule

The company has a training center responsible for training newly hired technicians to certify them for machine repair. A newly hired service engineer has to go through a one-week training course (initially) in which they learn the basics of the machine, how to order parts, how to fix the machine, and troubleshoot common errors. Some handpicked engineers undergo advanced training for an additional week to learn how to troubleshoot complex problems.

Typically, engineers must attend one of the scheduled training courses on the machine models they are hired to repair.

If an engineer does not get a training course right away, they are typically tagged along with a senior engineer to learn some common tasks and perform a few things within their capability and experience. Some engineers are hired from their competitor companies and typically may have better skills to repair the machines with minimal or no training.

TRAINING IMPACT MEASUREMENT

Case study

In a calendar year within the scope of this case study, a training influx looked like this: For the sake of simplicity, only two phases of hiring are shown. The first phase hired 20 technicians in the last Q4 and trained them within the same quarter. The second phase hired 35 technicians in Q1, 30 of whom were trained in Q2 and 5 in Q3.

The new technicians take about one quarter to become proficient after training. Thus, for those trained in Q4, their performance was measured in the following quarter Q1, not in the quarter during which they received training. During Q1, the performance of seasoned and newly trained technicians was measured separately.

In the next quarter, Q2, they are no longer considered newly trained and are counted as seasoned technicians. Thus, the seasoned technicians' count is 270.

The training assessment and measurement schedule looked as shown in Table 10 over a span of 5 quarters.

This adjustment continued quarter-over-quarter and worked perfectly for the nature of business and the typical time technicians took to reach the desired proficiency.

CH 9 – APPLYING THE MODEL IN PRACTICE

The target population in this case study

The population of interest for this case study is 30 technicians who got trained in Q2. This is the segment for which training impact and effectiveness are demonstrated using the ROE model.

Table 10: Training and measurement schedule

Quarter	Last	Current CY			
	Q4	Q1	Q2	Q3	Q4
Hired	20	35	-	-	-
Trained	20	-	30	5	-
Pre-training assessment	20	-	30	5	-
Post-training assessment	20	-	30	5	-
Supervisor's post-training assessment	-	20	-	30	-
Job performance measurement (seasoned)	250	250	270	270	300
Job performance measurement (newly trained)	-	20	-	30	5
Compute			RI	II, EI	

TRAINING ROI CHALLENGE

Training required substantial investment and travel expenses for the technicians. It was absolutely imperative for training managers and heads to ensure that training programs were highly effective and good use of the company's money. Thus, the organization had a similar challenge as described in the book. They needed to measure the effectiveness of training to defend the training ROI to their executives.

TE measurement challenge

The company has tried traditional models to present training ROI for several years. However, in their own words, they have not been very successful in making a case. Every annual review raised more questions about the relevance, effectiveness, and ROI of several training programs. As a result, over the years, they had to curtail their training programs in terms of offering, duration, and structure.

Eventually, they worked with me and decided to use the ROE methodology to address their challenge. In this case study, I will show you a condensed version of the 6-step data collection methodology and how they measured training effectiveness without inventing new processes or data pointers.

Let's first talk about the 6 steps of data collection flow.

CH 9 – APPLYING THE MODEL IN PRACTICE

STEP 1: COMPETENCY MAP FROM JOB PERFORMANCE METRICS

Step 1a: Job performance metrics

Before:

Their job performance metrics were 'Customer satisfaction scores: 4.5 out of 5.0 quarterly.'

The problem with this metric was that several engineers focused just on satisfying the customers. To do so, they preemptively ordered several 'just-in-case' expensive machine parts typically required in most common cases to fix a down machine. On other occasions, they spent many days trying to fix more straightforward problems. Customer satisfaction scores increased when customers saw the engineers doing everything well-planned, like bringing a bunch of parts to the site beforehand.

However, in the long run, the company observed the expenses on parts and labor going up, and their margins on the contracts shrank because engineers were not sensitive about the parts costs and hours spent on the cases.

TRAINING IMPACT MEASUREMENT

After:

After applying the ROE model, they re-looked at job performance metrics in line with organizational goals. They established new measures:

A. Case resolved successfully: Indicated engineers' success rate. The target is 80%.
B. Average time to resolve per case: Indicated proficiency of engineers. The target is 6 hours per case.
C. The average cost of parts per case: Indicated profitability. Target is $1000 per case.
D. The average cost of labor, including travel costs per head: Indicated proficiency of engineers. Target is $2000 per case.
E. Average customer satisfaction score: Indicated customer retention and future potential. The target is 4.5 of 5.0 per customer.

The new job performance metrics aligned well with the department's revenue, profitability, and customer base goals. The five job performance metrics are summarized in Table 11 with the target and weightage that was applied to each KPI.

Table 11: Job performance metrics

Job performance Metrics		Target	Weightage
A.	Case resolution success rate	80%	0.1
B.	Average time to resolve per case	6 hours	0.2

CH 9 - APPLYING THE MODEL IN PRACTICE

C.	Average cost of parts ordered/used per case	$1000	0.2
D.	Average labor cost (including travel costs) per case	$2000	0.2
E.	Average customer satisfaction scores	4.5	0.3

As suggested in previous chapters, this performance is measured based on multiple KPIs. They needed to combine these KPIs into a single number to compare and compute the Effectiveness Index.

The company chose a balanced scorecard (BSC) method in which they assigned the scoring brackets to each KPI based on the level of achievement. Then they assigned weightage to each KPI based on its importance to the company's strategic goals. The BSC scoring criteria are shown in Table 12.

Table 12: Job performance metrics

Balanced scorecard scoring	Score	Weightage
Exceed the target	120%	0.1
Achieved the target	100%	0.2
Up to 20% missed the target	80%	0.2
Between 20% to 40% missed the target	60%	0.2
More than 40% missed the target	0%	0.3

As you can see from the weight, the organization continued to emphasize customer satisfaction and the number of cases

TRAINING IMPACT MEASUREMENT

resolved. However, they emphasized parts and costs-related KPIs which were missing before.

With these metrics, they could review skill maps and messaging while ensuring their technicians knew what they were supposed to deliver.

Step 1b: Skills and knowledge competency

In that company, the HR department and training managers had been working together to create a competency map for that job role. However, in most instances, it was derived from their job description or similar templates that specified generic responsibilities.

Before:

Before using the ROE model, the job competency list they had been using is shown in Table 13.

Table 13: Job competencies identified before using the ROE model

Competencies (before the ROE model)
Understand the basics of photocopier machines
Understand how photocopier function works
Review product roadmaps and models and compare their features
Understand common specifications
Understand how to power up and down the machine
Understand the most common issues
Execute preventive maintenance of the machine

CH 9 - APPLYING THE MODEL IN PRACTICE

Learn how to replace parts A, B, C, and D
Learn what to do before handing the machine to the customer

This is just an excerpt. But most of the remaining ones also read on those lines. The training course designed with the above competency map was about one week long, 2-3 days of which were spent reviewing manuals, slides, and other informational material. However, there was continuous feedback on the ineffectiveness of training as new engineers kept struggling to get good customer satisfaction scores. The reason here is that the training competencies were hardly preparing them for what was expected.

After:

Then they applied the ROE model and started with the outcomes.

As part of the ROE model, first, they built the proficiency statement based on "What does the expected success look like for this job role?" After several rounds of deliberations, they formed the following proficiency statement:

Resolve a case within 6 average hours, ensure average part cost <$1000 and labor cost <$2000 at an 80% success rate, and attain a customer satisfaction score of 4.5 out of 5.0 across all cases.

Based on those outcomes, they worked backward and figured that they needed to give them the following essential capabilities, as shown in the excerpt in Table 14:

TRAINING IMPACT MEASUREMENT

Table 14: Job competencies identified by using the ROE model

Competencies (with ROE model)
Forecast parts and material needed based on symptoms
Order correct material, conserving costs
Work out the part costs and learn techniques to reduce costs
Compute estimated duration to resolve problems of various nature
How to shorten the time-to-resolution
How to balance customer satisfaction and contract profits
Analyze and interpret machine error codes
Assess non-parts and parts-based repair
Practice troubleshooting flow charts and identify optimal paths
Workout two tiers of repair plan if needed
Implement short-term stop-gap actions for long-lead repairs
Implement long-term permanent actions
Validate machine performance
Qualify as per specifications and contract agreements

The full list covered several skills ensuring that it lined up with the outcomes. No irrelevant skill was included in that list that was not leading to the outcomes.

Based on these perfectly aligned competencies, the training duration for most machine models was revised to 2 weeks.

A competency map derived from the outcomes is shown in Figure 18. This figure conveys how the competencies were worked out from the outcomes or proficiency statements and then linked in reverse.

CH 9 - APPLYING THE MODEL IN PRACTICE

Figure 18: Competency map derived from outcomes

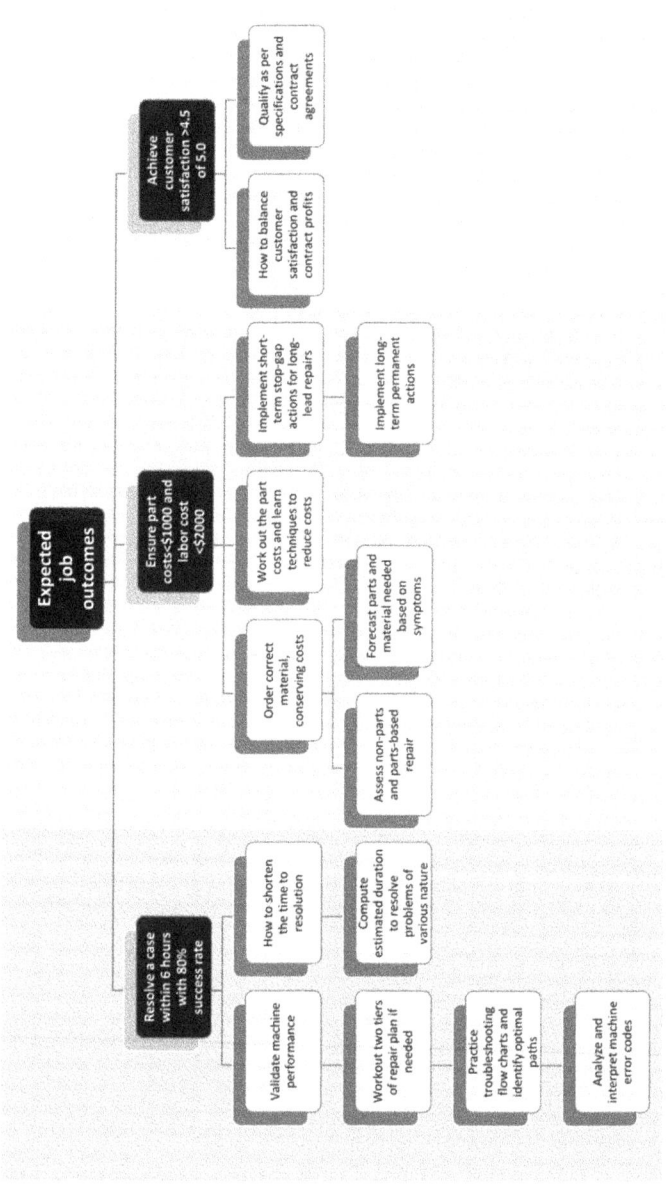

TRAINING IMPACT MEASUREMENT

STEP 2: PRE-TRAINING BASELINE

Step 2a: Last quarter's business performance metrics

The business performance data was readily available since the organization used to regularly review its operations, including finances, revenue, profitability, and other operational metrics.

Executives measured the performance of the sales and service department based on the following 7 KPIs:

1. Last quarter's service revenue allocation: Annual upfront payments, renewals during the quarter, and new sign-ups split into 4 equal parts and allocated to each quarter.
2. Last quarter's service contract profitability was prorated from the applicable duration from #1, and expenses paid to serve the contract (#3 and #4).
3. The total parts cost spent during the last quarter to serve the contracts.
4. Total person-hours and associated hourly costs spent during the last quarter (including travel time) to serve the contracts.
5. Customer satisfaction scores during the last quarter.
6. Service profitability per head during the last quarter (#2 divided by the total number of technicians).
7. Time-to-resolution during the last quarter and quarter-over-quarter improvement.

Executives had a good perception that training investment directly or indirectly impacted all 7 KPIs. However, the difficulty was in showing the linkage to business performance. How much impact was contributed by training? This question could hardly be answered using traditional methods. Or at least those methods were cumbersome to use in this context.

The above quarterly data became a business performance for the last quarter and was deemed as a baseline. As part of the ROE, it is recommended to identify a specific quarter's data as a baseline. This baseline better be based on the immediately preceding quarter's data.

Regarding training measurement, your goal is to beat or achieve what you achieved in the last quarter. That is the foundational principle of 'return on expectations' – to meet or beat the expectations you already established in the last quarter.

Step 2b: Pre-training assessment

The competency map above was converted into a self-assessment checklist whose criteria were to assess their confidence and competence. In this business context, the confidence scale was worked out as follows:

> A score of 1: I have done it under someone
> A score of 2: I have done it solo

In contrast, the competence scale was:

TRAINING IMPACT MEASUREMENT

A score of 1: 1 x performed
A score of 2: 2x performed
A score of 3: 3x performed

The pre-training assessment survey was sent to all the new employees slated to receive training. For example, in the Q2 snapshot, 30 technicians completed the pre-training assessment. Then, the scores were averaged across all new employees yet to receive the training. These scores were segmented for confidence and competence. They scored 0.5 on confidence and 0.3 on competence, as summarized in Table 15. The result showed that most of them were fresh to the photocopier industry or the company's products. They needed systematic training to become better at their skills.

The averaged quarterly scores for confidence and competence became the pre-training assessment baseline.

Table 15: Pre-training self-assessment of new technicians

Pre-training self-assessment, 30 technicians, Q2		
Competencies	Confidence (score 1 to 2)	Competence (score 1 to 3)
Forecast parts and material needed based on symptoms	0.3	0.1
Order correct material, conserving costs	0.35	0.2
Work out the part costs and learn techniques to reduce costs	0.32	0.3
Compute estimated duration to resolve problems of various nature	0.7	0.2

CH 9 - APPLYING THE MODEL IN PRACTICE

How to shorten the time-to-resolution	0.2	0.4
How to balance customer satisfaction and contract profits	1.3	0.4
Analyze and interpret machine error codes	1.2	0.5
Assess non-parts and parts-based repair	0.5	0.5
Practice troubleshooting flow charts and identify optimal paths	0.6	0.2
Workout two tiers of repair plan if needed	0.6	0.6
Implement short-term stop-gap actions for long-lead repairs	0.25	0.1
Implement long-term permanent actions	0.2	0.2
Validate machine performance	0.5	0.3
Qualify as per specifications and contract agreements	0.1	0.3
Average	**Avg confidence scores =0.5**	**Avg competence scores =0.3**

Step 2c: Baseline job performance of technicians

They already had a sound system for capturing technicians' onsite activities. To make things more efficient, they deployed a better CRM system to capture key onsite activity indicators (a subset of business performance KPIs) during each service case. This data was aggregated across all the technicians and segmented separately for seasoned (Table 16) vs. new technicians (Table 17). Note that the newly trained technicians at this point were 20 technicians hired in Q4 and trained in the same quarter.

With reference to the total number of cases logged in the last quarter, the organization measured five job performance

TRAINING IMPACT MEASUREMENT

metrics outlined in Step 1a and marked them as the latest baseline.

As an example, at the end of Q1, they baselined the performance of 250 fully qualified seasoned technicians.

Table 16: Job performance baseline of seasoned technicians

End of Q1 Job Performance Baseline, 250 seasoned technicians				
Job performance Metrics	Seasoned (250)	Target	Weight	BSC
Total number of cases logged in the last quarter	2900	-	-	-
A. Case resolution success rate	2500 (86%)	80%	0.1	120%
B. Average time to resolve per case	5 hours	6 hours	0.2	120%
C. Average cost of parts ordered/used per case	$1200	$1000	0.2	80%
D. Average labor cost (including travel costs) per case	$2100	$2000	0.2	80%
E. Average customer satisfaction scores	4.78	4.5	0.3	120%

This weighted BSC score for seasoned technicians' performance: $0.1*1.2+0.2*1.2+0.2*0.8+0.2*0.8+0.3*1.2= 0.92$ as the baseline.

At the end of the same quarter, they also had 20 newly trained technicians. They baselined their performance as they just got

CH 9 - APPLYING THE MODEL IN PRACTICE

trained the previous quarter, though it would not have shown significant change yet.

This weighted BSC score for newly trained technicians' performance: $0.1*1.2+0.2*0.8+0.2*0.6+0.2*0.6+0.3*1.0= 0.82$ as the baseline.

Table 17: Job performance baseline of newly trained technicians

End of Q1 Job Performance Baseline, 20 just-trained technicians				
Job performance Metrics	Newly trained (20)	Target	Weight	BSC
Total number of cases logged in the last quarter	250	-	-	-
F. Case resolution success rate	220 (88%)	80%	0.1	120%
G. Average time to resolve per case	7 hours	6 hours	0.2	80%
H. Average cost of parts ordered/used per case	$1400	$1000	0.2	60%
I. Average labor cost (including travel costs) per case	$2500	$2000	0.2	60%
J. Average customer satisfaction scores	4.5	4.5	0.3	100%

These two baselines acted as a reference of comparison for 30 technicians who would be trained in Q2.

TRAINING IMPACT MEASUREMENT

STEP 3: POST-TRAINING ASSESSMENT

Post-training self-assessment scores

At this step, they used the same checklist as in Step 2b and asked their newly trained technicians to fill it up. For instance, their Q1 snapshot had 35 technicians waiting for training. 30 of them got training in Q2. Those 30 were the target audience for this assessment. Depending upon the exact training dates, the general gap between the pre-assessment and post-training assessment varied from one month to three months. That period was reasonable to assimilate the skills learned in training. Some even got to do some of those tasks solo or under some mentor. Some got chances to practice the same task multiple times.

For the returned assessments, the scores were again segmented for confidence and competence. The averaged quarterly post-training scores for confidence and competence were then compared to the pre-training scores for the same participants.

The post-training assessment, for instance, in Q2, showed a confidence score of 1.7 and competence scores of 2.0 for 30 newly trained technicians. The post-training assessment is shown in Table 18.

CH 9 – APPLYING THE MODEL IN PRACTICE

Table 18: Post-training self-assessment of newly trained technicians

Post-training self-assessment, 30 technicians, Q2		
Competencies	Confidence (score 1 to 2)	Competence (score 1 to 3)
Forecast parts and material needed based on symptoms	1.5	2.3
Order correct material, conserving costs	1.9	2.4
Work out the part costs and learn techniques to reduce costs	1.8	2
Compute estimated duration to resolve problems of various nature	1.7	1.8
How to shorten the time-to-resolution	1.5	1.7
How to balance customer satisfaction and contract profits	2.3	2
Analyze and interpret machine error codes	2.2	2.1
Assess non-parts and parts-based repair	1.5	2.3
Practice troubleshooting flow charts and identify optimal paths	1.6	1.8
Workout two tiers of repair plan if needed	1.6	2
Implement short-term stop-gap actions for long-lead repairs	1.5	1.7
Implement long-term permanent actions	1.7	1.8
Validate machine performance	1.5	2.1
Qualify as per specifications and contract agreements	1.6	1.9
Average	Avg confidence scores =1.7	Avg competence scores =2.0

TRAINING IMPACT MEASUREMENT

Reaction Index

The data from Step 2b and Step 3 generated a Reaction Index for confidence and competence.

$$\text{Confidence} = 1.7/0.5 = 3.4$$
$$\text{Competence} = 2.0/0.3 = 6.6$$
$$\text{Average Reaction Index} = 5.0$$

The Reaction Index is large, indicating that training effectively brought the right confidence and competence in the form of skills required to perform the job.

It is worth noting that the company did not ask the technicians about their reactions to training. Instead, they were asked about their reaction to the changes they had seen due to training. It is a far more practical method to establish objectivity.

STEP 4: POST-TRAINING SUPERVISOR'S ASSESSMENT

At this step, during the Q3 timeframe, the supervisors of those 30 technicians trained in Q2 (for instance) were asked to do an assessment.

CH 9 – APPLYING THE MODEL IN PRACTICE

Post-training supervisor's assessment

For this assessment, the exact same checklist was used by technicians to do pre- and post-assessment in Step 2b and Step 3, respectively.

However, this step was done by supervisors looking at these technicians' onsite or field performance post-training, one quarter after the training. Supervisors rated their confidence on a scale of 2 and competence on a scale of 3. An excerpt is shown in Table 19.

Table 19: Post-training supervisor assessment of newly trained technicians

Post-training supervisor assessment, 30 technicians, Q3		
Competencies	Confidence (score 1 to 2)	Competence (score 1 to 3)
Forecast parts and material needed based on symptoms	1.6	2.9
Order correct material, conserving costs	1.9	3
Work out the part costs and learn techniques to reduce costs	1.9	2.6
Compute estimated duration to resolve problems of various nature	1.7	3.1
How to shorten the time-to-resolution	1.5	2.3
How to balance customer satisfaction and contract profits	2.3	2.6
Analyze and interpret machine error codes	2.2	3.1
Assess non-parts and parts-based repair	1.9	2.9

TRAINING IMPACT MEASUREMENT

Practice troubleshooting flow charts and identify optimal paths	1.6	2.4
Workout two tiers of repair plan if needed	1.8	2.8
Implement short-term stop-gap actions for long-lead repairs	1.5	2.9
Implement long-term permanent actions	1.7	2.3
Validate machine performance	1.8	2.8
Qualify as per specifications and contract agreements	1.6	2.4
Average	**Avg confidence scores =1.8**	**Avg competence scores =2.7**

Supervisors used several instruments and sources to make ratings as objective as possible. Some of the sources they used included:

Confidence:

o   Stakeholder 360-degree feedback
o   Case notes and escalation histories
o   Customer complaints or feedback
o   Case analysis
o   Mentor's ratings and assessment
o   Trainer's feedback and assessment

Competence:

o   Case resolved successfully
o   Average time-to-resolution from CRM
o   Customer satisfaction scores
o   Average parts costs

CH 9 - APPLYING THE MODEL IN PRACTICE

- Average person-hour costs
- Departmental performance

Improvement Index

Supervisor's ratings averaged over the entire quarter for all the trainees turned out to be 1.8 and 2.7 for confidence and competence, respectively.

Data from this step generated an Improvement Index for both confidence and competence.

>   Confidence = 1.8/0.5 = 3.6
>   Competence = 2.7/0.3 = 9.0
>   Average Reaction Index = 6.6

The Improvement Index is much higher than Reaction Index, indicating that training was highly effective in inducting the expected improvement in the field performance in terms of confidence and competence seen by managers, customers, and stakeholders.

A point worth noting is that supervisors were not asked to give performance review ratings for the technician's performance, typically done during performance review cycles. Instead, they were asked to provide their observations against the same set of competencies used to design training, pre-training, and post-training self-assessment instruments.

TRAINING IMPACT MEASUREMENT

Thus, you have all the measurements tied to the same common anchor. Further, the data used thus far was the department's day-to-day operational data with slight customization, such as assessment checklists.

This exercise is repeated on a rolling basis at the end of each quarter. Though new employees are rated each quarter, the quarter-over-quarter data represents how well the workforce is improving overall.

STEP 5: QUARTERLY JOB PERFORMANCE

In step 5, the standard employee job performance is evaluated. However, it is done every quarter. The performance measures or metrics used at this stage were the same as the baseline performance that was conducted in Step 2c.

The CRMs captured the key onsite activity indicators on an ongoing basis as part of their standard operating procedure. The data were aggregated across all the technicians and segmented separately for seasoned vs. newly trained technicians quarterly.

Quarterly performance seasoned

For example, one of the snapshots at the end of Q3 was 270 (seasoned) and 30 (newly trained) technicians who served on service cases last quarter.

CH 9 - APPLYING THE MODEL IN PRACTICE

In this quarterly iteration, they have two separate datasets. One for seasoned (Table 19) and one for newly trained (Table 20).

Table 20: Quarterly job performance of seasoned technicians

End of Q3 Job Performance, 270 seasoned technicians				
Job performance Metrics	Seasoned (270)	Target	Weight	BSC
Total number of cases logged in the last quarter	3200	-	-	-
K. Case resolution success rate	3000 (93%)	80%	0.1	120%
L. Average time to resolve per case	5.5 hours	6 hours	0.2	120%
M. Average cost of parts ordered/used per case	$1000	$1000	0.2	100%
N. Average labor cost (including travel costs) per case	$1900	$2000	0.2	120%
O. Average customer satisfaction scores	4.6	4.5	0.3	120%

This weighted BSC scores for 270 seasoned technicians' performance: $0.1*1.2+0.2*1.2+0.2*1.0+0.2*1.2+0.3*1.2 = 1.16$.

Leaders factored that seasoned technicians' performance was improving not because of training but because of process improvement and other factors since they were trained several quarters ago.

TRAINING IMPACT MEASUREMENT

Quarterly performance newly trained

The significance of training and its impact is in relationship to the newly trained technicians. They observed the KPIs of newly trained technicians as shown in Table 21:

Table 21: Post-training supervisor assessment of newly trained technicians

End of Q3 Job Performance, 30 newly trained technicians			
Job performance Metrics	Newly trained (30)	Target	Weight	BSC
Total number of cases logged in the last quarter	320	-	-	-
P. Case resolution success rate	300 (93%)	80%	0.1	120%
Q. Average time to resolve per case	6 hours	6 hours	0.2	100%
R. Average cost of parts ordered/used per case	$1200	$1000	0.2	80%
S. Average labor cost (including travel costs) per case	$2200	$2000	0.2	80%
T. Average customer satisfaction scores	4.8	4.5	0.3	120%

This weighted BSC scores for 30 newly trained technicians' performance: $0.1*1.2+0.2*1.0+0.2*0.8+0.2*0.8+0.3*1.2 = 1.0$.

CH 9 - APPLYING THE MODEL IN PRACTICE

Effectiveness Index

Here

> Quarterly BSC of 270 seasoned technicians = 1.16
> Quarterly BSC of 30 newly trained technicians = 1.00

Previously, they baselined:

> Last baseline BSC of 250 seasoned technicians = 0.92
> Last baseline BSC of newly trained technicians = 0.82

To compute Effectiveness Index, they could do a total of 4 ratios, out of which 1 is an invalid ratio. These scenarios are shown in Table 22.

Table 22: Potential Effectiveness Index Scenarios

	Seasoned BSC	Newly trained BSC
Seasoned baseline	EI = 1.16/0.92 = 1.26 How well 250 in the field continued to coach 20 junior technicians to perform well	EI = 1.0/0.92 = 1.08 How well training equipped newly trained 30 to perform close to seasoned 250 population
Newly trained baseline	Invalid	EI = 1.0/0.82 = 1.22 How well training equipped 30 newly trained population to at

TRAINING IMPACT MEASUREMENT

		least perform close to the previous 20 of similar population

As you see, the Effectiveness Index in all three scenarios is > 1, which means training has been highly effective in the classroom settings to develop the performance of newly trained technicians better than or similar to previous training quality.

At the same time, it seems senior guys in the field are inducting new juniors very well. As a result, the newly inducted population is becoming proficient faster.

STEP 6: QUARTERLY BUSINESS PERFORMANCE

The business performance data, which was gathered on a quarterly basis, is described under Step 2a. It was gathered for 7 KPIs as listed there.

The improvement in business performance quarter-over-quarter for those selected KPIs conveys the impact of training.

As a general approach, the organization used the balanced scorecard to compute one number that conveys the 7 KPIs collectively. They used a similar weighted system as described in this chapter. That way, they achieved a BSC score for baseline in Step 2a and quarterly BSC in Step 6. The ratio of quarterly BSC with baseline BSC resulted in Impact Index.

While the illustration of actual numbers is skipped here, the organization found an Impact Index of 1.3, indicating training alongside other process improvements positively impacted the business KPIs.

It must be noted that one quarter might be too less of a period to see the impact of training. However, when organizations follow this quarterly regime, they do not leave the computations for annual reviews. Instead, constant measurements out of readily available day-to-day data become part of their SOP.

RECAP

In this case study, we found that the organization worked out the following 4 indexes, summarized in Table 23.

Table 23: 4 Summary of 4 types of indices

Index	Value	Interpretation
Reaction Index (RI)	Post-training self-assessment vs pre-training self-assessment = 5.0	Training significantly influenced the confidence and competence of new technicians

TRAINING IMPACT MEASUREMENT

Improvement Index (II)	Post-training supervisor assessment vs pre-training assessment = 6.6	Training resulted in significantly observable performance
Effectiveness Index (EI)	Newly trained performance vs seasoned performance = 1.08 Newly trained vs previously trained performance = 1.22	Training given to new technicians is highly effective in delivering the required performance
Impact Index	Quarterly business BSC vs baseline BSC = 1.3	Training has impacted key business KPIs positively

As a training executive, you expect that training should improve new as well as previously newly trained technicians close to the established seasoned technicians.

10

FINAL THOUGHTS

TRAINING IMPACT MEASUREMENT

Effective training programs are essential for organizations to improve employee skills, knowledge, and job performance. However, measuring the effectiveness, impact, and ROI of training programs is equally important.

Admittedly, there are many models for TE/TI/TROI measurement. While there are some common fundamental premises among all those models, including the one presented in this book, the most important thing for any TE measurement is to relate the measurement metrics and processes with the business needs.

The traditional methods of measuring TE, such as Kirkpatrick's model, focus on measuring reaction, learning, behavior, and results. While these models provide a framework for measuring TE, they have several limitations. For example, these models do not consider the impact of training on the organization's business goals or the long-term impact of training. Additionally, these models rely heavily on subjective evaluations and do not provide a comprehensive view of the training program's impact.

In contrast, the ROE model provides a more practical and comprehensive approach to measuring a training program's TE/TI/TROI. The ROE model focuses on four tiers: reaction, learning, improvement, and effectiveness. This model also considers the impact of training on an organization's business goals and provides a quantitative approach to measuring the ROI of training programs.

CH 10 - FINAL THOUGHTS

The first tier of the ROE model measures the participants' immediate *reaction* to the training program. The second tier measures the *improvement* in terms of the extent to which participants have acquired the knowledge, skills, and attitudes taught in the training program. The third tier measures the *effectiveness* of training program on the employees' job performance indicators. The fourth tier measures the *impact* of training program on the organization's business goals.

This model has the scope for flexible application, scalability, and adaptations based on business needs, and it recommends no hard-and-fast rules. The model's four tiers provide a holistic view of training program's impact, from immediate reactions to long-term business impact. It also provides a quantitative approach to measuring the ROI of training programs, which is essential for organizations to justify the cost of training programs.

The ROE model's usability can be enhanced using a systematic data collection and analysis approach. The data should be collected from various sources, such as the organization's customer relationship management database, escalation matrix, task trackers, customer satisfaction scores, stakeholder 360-degree feedback, project success sheets, balanced scorecards, and employee performance data sources. This data can be consolidated to form a composite picture of the training program's impact on the organization's business goals.

The ROE model's implementation requires a significant investment of time and resources. However, the benefits of

TRAINING IMPACT MEASUREMENT

measuring TE/TI/TROI outweigh the costs. Measuring TE/TI/TROI helps organizations identify improvement areas in training programs, demonstrate their value to stakeholders, and justify their costs.

11
CAREER ACCELERATION RESOURCES

TRAINING IMPACT MEASUREMENT

LEARN FROM POWER-PACKED BOOKS

Accelerate your training thought leadership! Purchase these books at **amazon.com/author/raman.k.attri**.

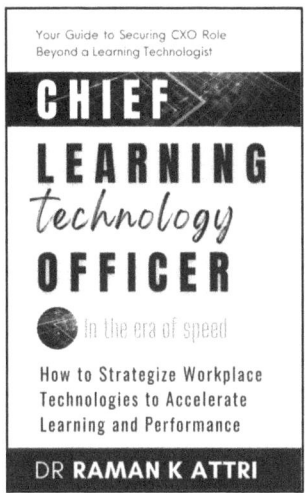

CAREER ACCELERATION RESOURCES

Chief Learning Technology Officer in the Era of Speed

Written for senior learning technology leaders who want to shine as CXO executives. This book describes five strategies to leverage current technologies to shorten time-to-proficiency and provides leaders with a framework to evaluate future technologies to impact employee development speed. You will walk out with an integrated system thinking about measuring, tracking, and reducing time-to-proficiency while integrating time-to-proficiency metrics as technology KPIs

Chief e-Learning Officer in the Era of Speed

Written for senior e-learning and training leaders who want to shine as CXO executives. The book describes five strategies to institute breakthrough e-learning to shorten time-to-proficiency. This book provides multi-level tips and operational tactics to implement these strategies. You will walk out with an integrated system thinking about a holistic e-learning ecosystem, which indeed can shorten time-to-proficiency metrics.

Iconic Chief Learning Officer

Written for visionary training and learning leaders to guide them through a breakthrough framework to become a globally recognized iconic chief learning officer. This book teaches the art and science of impactful corporate learning leadership above and beyond your job and your organization. Learn the secrets of accelerating your career to unimaginable heights.

Releasing 2024

Designing Training to Shorten Time to Proficiency

Written for training designers, this book delivers over 21 training and learning strategies across online learning, classroom instructions, and on-the-job learning that can enable designing workplace training programs to shorten the time to proficiency of employees. The book provides practical guidance for implementation to equip corporate learning specialists, HR professionals, training leaders, performance consultants, and direct managers. (Released)

TRAINING IMPACT MEASUREMENT

ENROLL IN ONLINE TRAINING COURSES

Accelerate your learning, training, and technology leadership with the following powerful online courses. For more such courses, head out to **get-there-faster.com/courses**.

L&D Leader and Strategist: Your Learning Leadership Accelerated

The learning, training, and development space is overcrowded and highly competitive now. Establishing yourself as a distinguished L&D leader is not easy anymore. You need to adopt a specific thought process and proven strategies to speed up your path to becoming a top L&D leader with unique specialization, positioning, and credibility. In this online course, learn the science of accelerating the path to becoming a top-notch learning and training leader. Master strategies, methods, and frameworks to put yourself onto the world map at an accelerated rate.

Enroll at **get-there-faster.com/learning-leadership-course**.

Speed Learner: Accelerated Learning Skill in the Era of Speed

Have you ever wished to learn anything faster in your profession or business? You get overwhelmed by a humongous amount of content, tasks, activities, and projects to master. You do not know where to start. The end result is that it takes you a long time, sometimes years, to master everything you have to do in your job. You tried all possible methods, but you did not see a difference in your learning speed. More often, professionals and leaders are at a loss to set the appropriate goals for their speedier learning and then achieve them at a faster rate. In this course, you will gain breakthrough insights on how to position your approaches to learn faster for professional goals and set yourself apart from your peers. In this course, you will learn how someone is viewed as a fast learner by most organizations. In this course, you will learn a breakthrough technique from Dr. Raman to accelerate your learning for professional success in your profession or job.

Enroll at **get-there-faster.com/speed-learning-course.**

Training Designer: Learn Powerful e-learning Design Practices to Speed Up Learning

Do you need to design online/e-learning courses to speed up the skill acquisition of your learners, but you don't know where to start? Life-changing skills are delivered when you design online or e-learning courses systematically using instructional design practices and using the latest and greatest strategies. In this training course, you will learn a new framework to think about your e-learning training design. You will walk out with proven, practical e-learning training design strategies from research used by some of the most advanced training organizations across the world. You will learn 3 key elements of e-learning design that you should pay attention to. You will also learn 5 strategies to make your e-learning courses powerful. You will adopt a new perspective on implementing 5 guiding principles in your e-learning or online courses.

Enroll at **get-there-faster.com/elearning-design-course.**

Strategize Technologies to Speed Up Employee Development

The speed with which teams are developed is far more critical now to meet the challenges of complex next-generation projects amidst a fast-paced business environment. Technologies are now the first line of defense to impact how employees learn, develop, and perform at a workplace. In this revolutionary course, you will receive first-hand research-based wisdom on an integrated system thinking approach to measuring, tracking, and reducing time-to-proficiency using analytics strategically. You will acquire a renewed business acumen for marrying two things - 'workforce analytics' and 'time-to-proficiency metrics'- to build a people analytics strategy that can ensure improving employee performance faster. You will learn how futuristic-thinking organizations have leveraged state-of-the-art technologies, analytics, tools, and systems to shorten the time-to-proficiency of the workforce and teams at the speed of business.

Enroll at **get-there-faster.com/strategic-technologies-course.**

TRAINING IMPACT MEASUREMENT

Artificial Intelligence for Enterprise Learning

Are you an executive or enterprise leader looking to implement AI and ChatGPT in your organization? Look no further! In this FREE course, structured around real demos of 25 different elements of AI and ChatGPT for corporate applications, you will be taken through the evolution of this breakthrough technology. You will learn how AI and ChatGPT can revolutionize how your organization can design, develop, and manage large-scale training programs, e-learning solutions, and knowledge management processes. You will also see how ChatGPT can assist in writing procedures and managing your entire corporate e-learning and knowledge management supply chain. You will shake up your traditional thinking and open your mind about how you can take such a powerful tool to your upper management and shine as a visionary leader. Enroll at **get-there-faster.com/enterprise-ai**.

GET CERTIFIED IN THE SCIENCE OF SPEED

Supercharge your learning leadership career to new heights by getting certified through a master certification program. For more such certifications, head out to **get-there-faster.com/pathways**.

Xcelerated Learning Strategist Certification: Speed-Savvy Chief Learning Officer

Designed for learning and training specialists, training managers, L&D professionals, human resources executives, and coaches to help them shine as world-class, speed-savvy learning thought leaders. This certification is awarded through rigorous training and qualification to develop the participants as the world's top-notch experts on accelerated learning in organizational space. Based on two decades of research, experience, experimentation, and authoring, this certification is structured around 5 power-packed tracks to qualify ambitious learning specialists who want to master the science of speed in learning, training, performance, and employee development.

To apply for acceptance to this certification, check out **get-there-faster.com/xcelerated-learning-guru-pathway.**

Xcelerated Training Design Guru Certification: Speed-Savvy Training Officer

Designed for learning and training specialists, training professionals, trainers, instructional designers, speakers, coaches, and teachers to help them shine as highly sought-after training design strategists. This certification is awarded through rigorous training and qualification to develop the participants as the world's top-notch experts in designing complex training and mentoring programs. If you need to equip your learners and audience with complex skills and improve their performance faster, then this advanced certification is for you. Based on two decades of research, experience, experimentation, and authoring, this certification is structured around 5 power-packed tracks to teach you the breakthrough, advanced, integrated methodologies for start-to-end analysis, design, development, and delivery of your training programs. Take your learning design to the next level by mastering the design of transformational coaching, mentoring, and certification programs.

To apply for acceptance to this certification, check out **get-there-faster.com/xcelerated-training-guru-pathway.**

INSIGHTFUL KEYNOTES FOR YOUR EVENTS

Interested to book me for powerful, insightful, research-backed, revolutionary keynotes and talks that will change your executives' thinking process? Then head on to **get-there-faster.com/speaking** and book me for your next corporate event. Book me and learn the science of acceleration to stay ahead in business!

REFERENCES

1. Attri, Raman K. 2005, "Return on Expectations (ROE): A Working Model for Measuring Effectiveness of Service Training," available at https://dx.doi.org/10.13140/RG.2.1.1085.5765 and https://www.researchgate.net/publication/285587862.
2. Kirkpatrick, DL & Kirkpatrick, JD 2009, Transferring Learning to Behavior: Using the Four Levels to Improve Performance, Berrett-Koehler.
3. Kirkpatrick Partners, (no date). The Kirkpatrick Model. https://www.kirkpatrickpartners.com/Our-Philosophy/The-Kirkpatrick-Model
4. Vance, A. 2017. The Bottomline on ROI: How to Measure the Results of Your Training, ROI Institute. https://roiinstitute.net/bottomline-roi-measure-results-training/
5. Brinkerhoff, R. O. (2003). The success case method: A strategic evaluation approach to increasing the value and effect of training. Advances in Developing Human Resources, 5(2), 132-151.
6. Jolivette, K., & Woo, S. E. (2018). Measuring the effectiveness of training: Challenges and best practices. OD Practitioner, 50(3), 16-22.
7. Leimbach, M. (2017). The challenges of evaluating training on a large scale. Training Industry Magazine, 59.
8. Noe, R. A. (2017). Employee training and development. McGraw-Hill Education.
9. O'Reilly, D., & Farndale, E. (2013). Evaluating human resource development: A toolkit for practitioners. Routledge.
10. Xie, Y., & Li, J. (2017). A deep learning approach to predicting the effectiveness of training programs. Journal of Educational Technology Development and Exchange, 10(1), 1-14.

REFERENCES

11. Brinkman, S., Simons, P. R. J., & Jochems, W. M. G. (2017). Evaluating technical training effectiveness: A systematic literature review. Human Resource Development Review, 16(3), 244-273.
12. Chen, Y. F., & Pan, M. L. (2013). Evaluating the effectiveness of technical training programs: An empirical study in Taiwan. Journal of Technical Education and Training, 5(1), 1-13.
13. Golaszewski, T., & Biddle, C. (2012). Evaluating the effectiveness of technical training: Practical recommendations for evaluation planning. Performance Improvement Quarterly, 25(3), 43-68.
14. Jackson, S., Malcolm, C., Sutherland, S., & Balan, P. (2015). Evaluating technical training effectiveness in the context of systems thinking. Proceedings of the Canadian Engineering Education Association (CEEA), 1-8.
15. Jaap, A., & Duckworth, V. (2014). Using a modified success case method to evaluate technical skills training: A case study in the UK nuclear industry. Evaluation and Program Planning, 47, 70-78.
16. Muijtjens, A. M. M., Hannon, F. B., Bakker, A. B., Schaafsma, F. G., van der Vleuten, C. P. M., & Beusmans, G. H. M. I. (2013). A competency-based model for technical skills assessment of residents in surgical training. Medical Education, 47(9), 904-912.
17. Pohlandt-McCormick, L., & Kazanas, H. C. (2019). Technical training effectiveness: A research synthesis. Industrial and Commercial Training, 51(1), 6-13.
18. Stolovitch, H. D., & Keeps, E. J. (2011). Handbook of human performance technology: Principles, practices, and potential. John Wiley & Sons.

INDEX

A

ability 73, 85
accelerated resolution 127
achievements 5, 8, 26, 114, 134
acquisition 7–8, 53
   acquisition of knowledge 7–8
aggregated 77, 114, 142, 151
algorithms 45–46
analysis 8, 25, 27, 35–36, 44, 53, 55, 67–68, 72–73, 121, 149, 162
   analysis approach 162
   analysis exercise 121
   analysis methods 36
   analysis of a sales job 73
analytics 40, 43–45, 47, 53, 68
assessing 5–8, 18–19, 22–23, 25–27, 61, 67, 74, 77, 109, 137, 140, 142, 146, 148
   assessing learners 109
   assessing the economic impact 8
   assessing the outcomes 7–8
assessments 7–8, 22, 27, 33–34, 37, 44–47, 68–69, 81, 92–93, 99, 104–5, 109–10, 129–30, 140–41, 145, 147–49, 151, 153, 156–57
averaged 69, 75–77, 79–80, 82–83, 120, 141, 145, 150

B

balanced 83–84, 100–101, 114, 134, 155, 162
   balanced scorecard 83–84, 100–101, 114, 134, 155, 162
   balanced scorecard process 84, 114
   balanced scorecard scoring 134
baseline 68, 74–79, 81, 85, 87, 91–92, 95, 104, 109, 111, 113, 119, 122, 139–44, 151, 154–55, 157
baseline a specific quarter 77
baseline average 122
baseline data 74, 85, 113, 119, 122
baseline for business performance 78
baseline for the self-assessment 78
baseline job performance 142
baseline measurements 111
baseline newly trained population 154
baseline of seasoned technicians 143
baseline performance 74–76, 151
baseline performance of employees 74
baseline reference 79, 81
baseline scores 91–92, 95
baseline self-assessment 77, 91, 95, 104
baseline self-assessment score 95, 104
baseline self-assessment survey 91
baseline threshold 75
behavior 10, 12, 46, 60, 100, 161
benefits 6–8, 21–22, 48–49, 162
   benefits of training 6–7, 21–22, 162
blueprints 71
Brinkerhoff 10, 14, 18, 44
business 5, 31–32, 38, 44, 47, 49, 51–56, 59–62, 67–69, 74–75, 78–79, 82, 84, 86–87, 92–93, 95, 101, 104, 110, 113, 119–22, 127–29, 139–40, 142, 155–57, 161–62
   business acumen 49
   business approach 113
   business context 55, 140
   business contributor 113
   business-driving 122
   business goals 51–52, 59, 74, 161–62
   business impact 32, 87, 162
   business indicators 104, 121
   business KPIs 120–21, 156–57
   business managers 49, 51–55, 67–68
   business metrics 56, 101, 119
   business model 62, 122

INDEX

business needs 61, 93, 95, 113, 128, 161–62
business objectives 5, 119
business operations 31, 82
business organizations 86
business outcomes 38, 44, 47, 54, 60–61
business performance 53, 59, 61, 68–69, 74, 78, 86, 113, 119, 139–40, 142, 155
   business performance indicators 74, 86
   business performance KPIs 142
   business performance metrics 61, 139
business reporting 86
business result 86, 104, 120
business unit performance 69, 87

C

capability 128
capable 40–41
   capable of handling 40
   capable of performing 41
challenge 22–26, 31–35, 40, 44, 48–51, 53–54, 67, 96, 130–31
challenging 23, 33–34, 36, 42, 52, 67
checklists 140, 145, 148, 151
classroom 40, 155
   classroom settings 155
   classroom training 40
collection 35, 44–45, 53, 67–68, 70, 78, 85, 92–95, 100–104, 110–12, 120–21, 123, 131, 162
   collection methodology 131
   collection methods 67
common-sense 56, 59
   common-sense methodology 59
   common-sense model 59
comparison-driven 55
competencies 36–39, 46, 72–73, 135–37, 141, 146, 148, 150
competency 43, 68, 71–74, 80, 83, 132, 135–38, 140
   competency-based 46
   competency list 135
   competency map 68, 71–74, 80, 83, 132, 135–38, 140

competency thinking 43
comprehensive 9, 14, 16, 18, 35, 37–38, 46–47, 53–54, 161
   comprehensive approach 37, 161
   comprehensive evaluation 18, 53–54
   comprehensive evaluation framework 53–54
   comprehensive framework 16
   comprehensive picture 38
   comprehensive understanding 9, 14, 18, 46–47, 54
   comprehensive view 161
computation 54, 68, 156
confidence 68, 74, 77, 80, 91, 93, 95, 100–101, 105, 140–42, 145–50, 156
cost-benefit analysis 8, 27
cost-effective 8, 27, 45, 54, 67
   cost-effective approach 45
costs-related KPIs 135
course 15, 40, 56, 67, 75–76, 101, 128, 136

D

data 22, 25–26, 32–33, 35, 40, 42–47, 53, 61, 67–71, 74–85, 87, 92–95, 100–104, 106, 109–13, 119–23, 131, 139–40, 142, 147, 150–51, 155–56, 162
   data accuracy 33
   data analytics 40, 44–45, 47, 53, 68
   data analytics exercise 68
   data baseline 78
   data collection 35, 44–45, 53, 67–68, 70, 85, 92–95, 100–104, 110–12, 120–21, 123, 131, 162
   data-driven 7, 110
   data inputs 100–101
   data management 33
   data overload 33, 43
   data pointers 131
   data privacy 42
   data sources 61, 81–84, 100, 110, 120, 162
   data technology 43
datasets 152
design 74, 114–15, 150
   design a pre-training rating 74
   design training 150

development 3, 25, 36, 40–41, 49, 53, 77, 80
   development gaps 80
   development process 3
dollar-based ROI 54

E

effectiveness 3–7, 18, 20–21, 27, 31, 34, 36, 39, 46–48, 50, 52, 54, 59–60, 75, 85, 101, 105, 109–16, 120, 122, 130–31, 134, 154–55, 157, 161–62
   effectiveness index 59–60, 85, 109–16, 120, 122, 134, 154–55, 157
   effectiveness indices 114
   effectiveness measurement 3, 34
   effectiveness of program 21, 27
   effectiveness of training 36, 46, 50, 52, 59, 109, 113, 131, 162
efficiency 22, 38, 41, 54
efficient 35, 62, 142
   efficient data collection 35
employees 5, 7, 21–22, 25, 35–36, 39–42, 59, 69, 73–77, 79–83, 85, 93, 104–5, 109–11, 113, 115, 127, 141, 151, 162
   employees' job 109, 162
   employees' performance 40
   employees' skills 41, 59, 105
   employees baseline 75–76
   employees effectiveness 115
   employees pre-training 74
engagement 19, 21, 25, 52
evaluation 3–4, 6–11, 14–15, 18, 21, 33, 36, 38, 43–44, 46, 53–54, 60, 161
   evaluation framework 53–54
   evaluation method 7–9, 36, 44
   evaluation model 11, 14–15, 18, 21, 33, 38, 44, 46, 53, 60
   evaluation plan 7
   evaluation process 36
evidence-based sources 82
expectations 23, 25, 27, 55–56, 59–60, 91, 93, 104, 111, 140
experience 15, 37, 73, 128

F

fast-paced changes 39
feedback-based mechanisms 54

feedback-driven process 61
financial-driven 55
five-level 12–13, 18
   five-level model 12–13, 18
   five-level ROI 13
four-level model 9–11, 18
framework 9–10, 16, 18, 52–54, 59–60, 62, 67–68, 161
   framework for data collection 68
   framework for evaluating 16, 52

G

guidelines 68

H

hands-on 37, 40
   hands-on exercises 40
   hands-on experience 37
higher-order technical skills 48

I

impact 3–23, 25–27, 31–35, 37–39, 41, 43–45, 47, 49, 51–56, 59–63, 67, 69, 71, 73, 75, 77, 79, 81–83, 85, 87, 91–93, 95, 99, 101, 103–5, 109–11, 113, 115, 119–23, 127, 129–31, 133, 135, 137, 139–41, 143, 145, 147, 149, 151, 153, 155–57, 161–63
   impact index 59–60, 87, 119, 121–23, 155–57
   impact measurement 3, 5, 7, 9, 11, 13, 15, 17, 19, 21, 23, 25, 27, 31, 33, 35, 37, 39, 41, 43, 45, 47, 49, 51, 53, 55, 59, 61, 63, 67, 69, 71, 73, 75, 77, 79, 81–83, 85, 87, 91, 93, 95, 99, 101, 103, 105, 109, 111, 113, 115, 119, 121, 123, 127, 129, 131, 133, 135, 137, 139, 141, 143, 145, 147, 149, 151, 153, 155, 157, 161, 163
   impact measures 10, 12, 59
   impact methodology 55
important 7, 9, 19–22, 50, 52, 77, 95, 109, 161
   important aspects 7
   important indicators 20–21, 52

INDEX

important measure 95
important thing 161
improvement 8, 21, 24–25, 59–61, 78, 83, 86, 91–92, 96, 99–106, 110, 114–16, 120, 139, 150, 152, 155–57, 161–63
  improvement in a training program 99
  improvement in attitudes 104
  improvement in business performance 155
  improvement in customer satisfaction 86
  improvement index 59–60, 83, 96, 99–100, 102–6, 110, 115–16, 120, 150, 157
  improvement index for a training 104
  improvement in employee performance 78
  improvement in employee retention rates 25
  improvement in employees' skills 59
  improvement in on-the-job skills 99–100
  improvement in perceived skills 91–92
  improvement in skills 105, 110
  improvement in the field performance 150
  improvement trends 61
index 59–62, 79, 81, 83, 85, 87, 91–96, 99–100, 102–6, 109–16, 119–23, 134, 147, 150, 154–57
indices 56, 68, 70, 87, 114, 120, 156
ineffectiveness of training 26, 136
influence 19–20, 100
instructional 5, 51
  instructional designers 5
  instructional technologies 51
instructor-led training 40
investment 3–4, 6, 8, 12, 31, 35, 48, 55–56, 60–61, 130, 140, 162
  investment-intensive training 48

J

job-specific results 110
justify the cost of training 162

K

Kirkpatrick 3, 9–12, 18, 52–53, 56, 60, 161
  kirkpatrick 4-level training evaluation 11
  kirkpatrick model 53
KPIs 84, 87, 114, 120–21, 134–35, 139–40, 142, 153, 155–57

L

large-scale 31–36, 39–45, 48, 52
  large-scale technical training 40–44
  large-scale training 31, 33–36, 42, 44–45, 48, 52
  large-scale training program 31, 33–36, 42, 44–45, 48, 52
leadership 19, 40
  leadership support 19
learners 4–5, 7–8, 10, 12, 14, 20, 93, 109, 114–15
  learners' acquisition 7–8
  learners' improvements 114–15
  learners' reaction 10, 12
  learners' reactions 109
  learners' skills 109
learning 3, 5, 9–10, 12, 14–15, 19–20, 23, 27, 38, 45, 49–51, 59–60, 105, 161
  learning experience 15
  learning improvement 60, 161
  learning objectives 5, 38
  learning outcomes 9, 19, 27
  learning styles 20
  learning transfer 14–15, 51
limitations 9–11, 13–14, 18, 21, 35, 46, 161
long-term 20, 23–24, 27, 53, 101, 137, 142, 146, 149, 161–62
  long-term business 162
  long-term effectiveness 101
  long-term effects 23–24, 27
  long-term impact 161
  long-term impact of training 161

M

machine 45, 127–28, 132, 135–37, 142, 146, 148–49
  machine learning 45
  machine models 128, 137

machine parts 132
machine performance 137, 142, 146, 149
machine problem 127
machine repair 128
management 33, 40, 53–54, 61, 82, 84, 100–101, 162
   management database 100–101, 162
   management model 54
   management processes 54
   management systems 82, 84
manager 5, 25, 48–49, 51–56, 67–68, 73, 77, 79, 81–82, 84–85, 92, 100, 106, 131, 135, 150
measurable 110, 114
   measurable improvements 114
measured 5–6, 11, 13, 75–76, 79, 84, 114, 122, 129, 131, 134, 139, 142
   measured by assessing 5–6
   measured by comparing 6
   measured the performance 139
   measured training effectiveness 131
measurement 3, 5, 7–9, 11, 13, 15, 17, 19–23, 25–27, 31–39, 41–43, 45–49, 51–55, 59–64, 67, 69, 71–73, 75, 77, 79, 81–85, 87, 91–93, 95–96, 99–101, 103–5, 109–11, 113, 115, 119–23, 127, 129–31, 133, 135, 137, 139–41, 143, 145, 147, 149, 151, 153, 155–57, 161, 163
measurement data 67, 121
measures 5–6, 9–12, 18–19, 21–24, 27, 31, 35–37, 39, 44, 51, 53–56, 59, 62, 67, 71, 82, 84, 91–93, 95, 99–101, 104, 106, 109–10, 113, 120, 131, 133, 151, 162
   measures the effectiveness 162
   measures the financial ROI 12
   measures the impact 10, 12, 109, 162
   measures the improvement 91, 162
   measures their readiness 93
   measures the relative improvement 59
   measures the training reaction 92
measuring 7–9, 22–26, 31–33, 35–38, 42–43, 48, 53–54, 56, 61, 67–68, 91–93, 99, 109–10, 112, 114, 116, 119, 161–63
   measuring the confidence 93

measuring the effectiveness 7, 36, 109, 161
measuring the impact 53, 119
measuring the ROI 161–62
measuring the worthiness 48
measuring trainees' reaction 92
measuring training impact 43, 119
measuring training ROI 8
methodology 54–56, 59, 131
methods 7–9, 34, 36, 40, 43–44, 67, 101, 119, 140, 161
model 9–18, 38, 44, 46, 53–56, 59–64, 67–68, 79, 81, 83, 85, 87, 91–92, 95–96, 99, 104–5, 109, 113, 119, 121–22, 130, 133, 135–37, 161–62

N

non-formative training 93
non-formative training assessments 93
non-technical skills 40
non-training 55
numerical representation 60

O

objective 4–5, 8–9, 26–27, 37–38, 44, 51–52, 61, 82, 85, 92–93, 99–100, 110–11, 115, 119–21, 149
   objective measure 92, 99–100, 110, 120
   objective measures 37, 44, 82
objectively 101
observations 8, 37, 150
one-size-fits-all approach 20
operational 139, 151
   operational data 151
   operational metrics 139
organizational 3–4, 6–12, 14, 19–21, 26–27, 45, 47, 51–53, 62, 83–84, 101, 105–6, 113, 120–21, 133
   organizational baseline 113
   organizational benefits 6
   organizational change 19
   organizational culture 19, 21
   organizational data 83
   organizational development 3
   organizational effectiveness 7
   organizational environment 9

INDEX

organizational goals 4, 8, 26, 51–52, 133
organizational impact 51
organizational metrics 7
organizational outcomes 8–12, 14, 20–21, 26–27, 45, 52–53
organizational performance 84, 120
organizational processes 47
organizational profit 121
organizational settings 101
organizational-specific 72
organizational standpoint 62
organizational strategy 9
organization-specific skills 76

P

parameters 109, 111, 121
performance 3, 5, 7, 20, 22–24, 26–27, 34–35, 37, 40, 46–47, 49–53, 59–62, 67–69, 71–76, 78, 81–87, 91, 93, 99–101, 104–6, 109–11, 113–16, 119–21, 129–30, 132–34, 137, 139–40, 142–44, 146, 148–53, 155, 157, 161–62
 performance data 61, 69, 75–76, 78, 81, 85, 87, 93, 100–101, 109–10, 119–21, 139, 155, 162
 performance goals 113
 performance improvement 99, 106, 150
 performance indicators 62, 69, 74–75, 84, 86, 109–11, 113, 115–16, 120, 162
 performance KPIs 142
 performance measurement 84, 130
 performance measures 151
 performance metric 47, 61, 67–68, 71–73, 75, 81, 83, 87, 132–34, 139, 143–44, 152–53
 performance numbers 113
 performance parameters 109, 111
 performance rating 82
 performance support 51, 105
personalized training 47
person-hours 113, 121, 139, 150
pre-assessment 145
preemptively 132

pre-training 68, 74, 77, 80–81, 85, 91–92, 95, 104, 109, 111, 113, 119, 122, 130, 139–41, 145, 150
 pre-training assessment 130, 140–41
 pre-training baseline 68, 74, 85, 91–92, 95, 104, 111, 119, 139
 pre-training exercise 111
 pre-training rating 74
 pre-training scores 145
 pre-training self-assessment 68, 74, 77, 141
 pre-training skills 95
 pre-training stage 80–81, 122
production 42
productive 113
productivity 3, 5, 7–8, 10, 12, 23, 26, 38, 41, 45, 54, 109, 111
professional 49, 73

Q

qualified 73, 127–28, 143
 qualified technicians 127
qualitative 14, 43–44, 53, 101
 qualitative approach 14
 qualitative evaluation 44
 qualitative measures 44, 53
quantifiable impact 110
quantified 49, 109, 113
 quantified assessment 109
 quantified figure 49
quantitative 19, 21, 43–44, 53, 93, 101, 161–62
 quantitative approach 161–62
 quantitative measures 19, 21
 quantitative methods 43–44
quarter-over-quarter 82, 129, 139, 151, 155

R

range 9, 19, 22, 38–40, 44, 54
rating 7, 74, 82, 91–92, 99, 101, 149–50
 rating data 82
 rating scores 92
 rating survey 74
reaction 10–12, 59–60, 79, 81, 91–96, 105–6, 120, 147, 150, 156, 161–62
 reaction measures 10, 12

requirements 42, 52, 54, 96, 105
results 8–12, 33, 60–61, 69, 72, 86, 92, 104, 110, 161
return-on-investment analysis 8, 25

S

satisfaction 5–7, 19, 22, 25–26, 41, 46, 48, 52, 59, 69, 83–84, 86, 100–101, 111, 132–34, 136–37, 139, 142–44, 146, 148–49, 152–53, 162
   satisfaction levels 5
   satisfaction score 133, 136
scale 32, 40, 67, 110, 140, 148
scorecards 83–84, 100–101, 114, 134, 155, 162
self-assessment 37, 68, 74, 77–78, 80–81, 91–92, 95, 104, 140–41, 145–46, 150
   self-assessment baseline 74, 78
   self-assessment checklist 140
   self-assessment data 77–78
   self-assessment instruments 150
   self-assessment rating 91–92
   self-assessment score 91, 95, 104, 145
   self-assessment survey 91, 95
self-reported surveys 37
short-term 20, 24, 53, 137, 142, 146, 149
   short-term improvements 24
   short-term outcomes 20, 53
   short-term stop-gap 137, 142, 146, 149
significant 3, 16, 19, 21, 33, 35, 144, 162
   significant challenges 33
   significant change 144
   significant impact 21
   significant investment 35, 162
   significant resources 3, 16
skill-building 53
skills 4–5, 7–8, 10, 12, 14, 16, 20, 22, 24, 32, 36–41, 46–48, 59, 68–69, 71–74, 76–77, 80–83, 91–93, 95, 99–101, 104–6, 109–11, 128, 135, 137, 141, 145, 147, 161–62
subjective 19, 36–37, 44, 82, 91, 93, 99, 101, 161
   subjective evaluations 161
   subjective expectations 93
   subjective factors 19
   subjective feedback 91

subjective measures 36–37
subjective rating 82
subjective ratings 99
success 10, 14, 18, 38, 44–45, 55, 61, 71, 83–84, 100–101, 111, 121, 133, 136, 143–44, 152–53, 162
   success rate 111, 121, 133, 136, 143–44, 152–53
supervisor 7, 69, 81–82, 100–101, 104, 110, 147–50, 153, 157
systems 43, 46–47, 51, 67, 72, 82, 84, 105
systems thinking 46–47

T

tasks 16, 36, 73, 77, 82, 84, 100–101, 128, 145, 162
task-specific 76
technicians 127–30, 135, 139, 141–48, 151–57
technological advances 9
technologies 51
technology 34, 36, 39, 43–44, 47, 53, 67
   technology analytics 43
   technology industries 36
   technology organizations 47
technology-savvy 31
threshold 75
time-constrained 35
time-consuming 14, 25–26, 36, 53, 67
time-to-resolution 48, 69, 83, 86, 111, 137, 139, 142, 146, 148–49
traditional 18, 21, 36–39, 46, 49, 51, 53–54, 60, 71–72, 91–92, 99, 109, 119, 131, 140, 161
   traditional approach 71–72
   traditional methodologies 54
   traditional methods 119, 140, 161
   traditional models 18, 36–37, 53, 91–92, 131
   traditional quantitative measures 21
   traditional ROI measurements 51
   traditional training 39, 49
   traditional training models 39
training 3–15, 17–27, 31–56, 59–63, 67–69, 71, 73–83, 85, 87, 91–93, 95–96, 99–101, 103–6, 109–11, 113–16, 119–23, 127–31, 133, 135–37, 139–41, 143, 145, 147–57, 161–63

INDEX

training alignment 95
training analysis 121
training assessment 93, 129, 157
training cases 44
training class 91–92
training competencies 136
training course 76, 128, 136
training dates 145
training delivery 34
training duration 137
training effectiveness 3–4, 18, 115, 131
training environment 34, 43
training evaluation 3–4, 11, 33, 53
training event 50, 79–80, 93
training experiences 47
training impact 3–5, 7, 9, 11, 13, 15, 17, 19, 21, 23, 25, 27, 31, 33, 35, 37, 39, 41, 43, 45, 47, 49, 51, 53, 55, 59–60, 63, 67, 69, 71, 73, 75, 77, 79, 81–83, 85, 87, 91, 93, 95, 99, 101, 103, 105, 109, 111, 113, 115, 119, 121, 123, 127, 129–31, 133, 135, 137, 139, 141, 143, 145, 147, 149, 151, 153, 155, 157, 161, 163
training improvement 105
training initiatives 51
training instructors 81
training intervention 50–51
training investment 60, 140
training leader 7
training managers 67, 81, 106, 135
training measurement 32, 140
training models 39
training needs 96
training objectives 51–52, 111, 115, 121
training outcomes 32
training participants 92
training program 3–10, 12–13, 17–27, 31–49, 51–56, 59, 61–62, 67, 74–75, 77–80, 85, 87, 91–93, 95–96, 99–101, 104–5, 109–10, 114–16, 119–21, 131, 161–63
training providers 34
training reaction 92
training records 45
training ROI 7–8, 49, 130–31

U

understanding 9, 14, 18, 27, 45–47, 54, 60, 72, 99, 135

V

validated 96

W

well-designed evaluation 7
well-drafted instrument 91–92
well-planned 132
well-trained employees 40–41

W

well-designed 3
well-drafted 87–88
well-planned 128
well-trained 36–37

FROM THE SAME AUTHOR

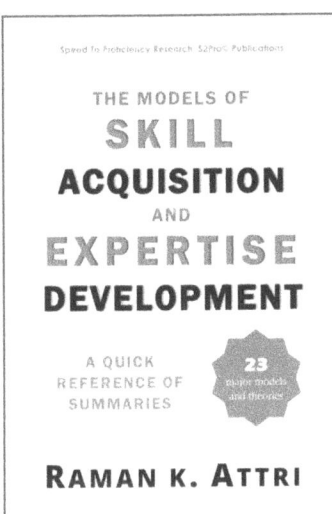

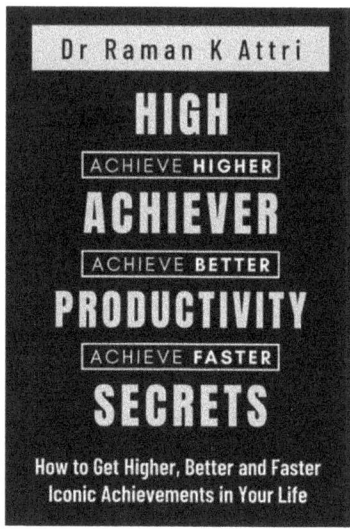

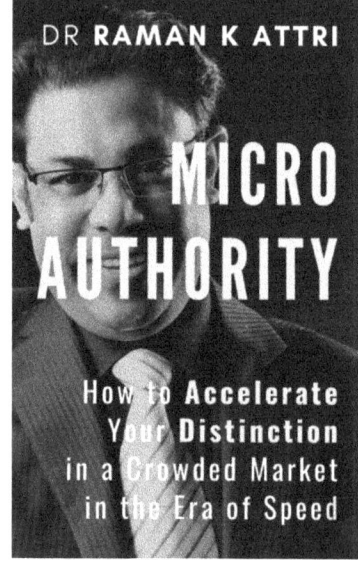

FROM THE COVER

This book provides a practical and intuitive model for measuring the effectiveness of technical training programs, addressing the challenges faced by technical training managers and other technical managers in justifying the return on investment for large-scale and investment-intensive training programs.

The 4-tier Return on Expectations (ROE) framework presented in this book, developed through years of research, observation, and experience, aims at reducing the pains of technical business managers while presenting and return on investment (ROI) of their training programs.

This book reduces your pains by eliminating the need to dollarize every piece of training investment. It also makes you less dependent on practically difficult methods to compute a defendable ROI. Instead, it will guide you on clarifying your and your stakeholders' expectations and then presenting a return on expectations, using the most relevant metrics and practical approach to calculate four indices: training reaction index, improvement index, effectiveness index, and impact index.

By using a feedback-based and data-driven approach, this book enables technical training managers or training leaders handling large-scale programs to collect data, measure key indicators, and compute indices that provide evidence of the effectiveness of their training programs, ultimately helping them communicate the value and effectiveness of your training programs to executives. Never again would you return to your traditional methods.

www.ingramcontent.com/pod-product-compliance
Lightning Source LLC
LaVergne TN
LVHW061532070526
838199LV00033B/638/J